WHITETAIL HUNTING

WHITETAIL HUNTING

Jim Dawson

Stackpole Books

Copyright © 1982 by Jim Dawson

Published by
STACKPOLE BOOKS
Cameron and Kelker Streets
P. O. Box 1831
Harrisburg, PA 17105

Printed in the U.S.A.

Library of Congress Cataloging in Publication Data

Dawson, Jim.
    Whitetail hunting.

    Includes index.
    1. White-tailed deer hunting. I. Title.
SK301.D375   799.2′77357   82-5661
ISBN 0-8117-1872-7   AACR2

I would like to dedicate this book to my family. Their love, understanding, and support make everything possible.

Contents

Acknowledgments

Many years of studying and hunting the whitetail deer under widely varying conditions made this book possible. But if it were not for the wonderful people at Stackpole Books, and particularly my editor, David Detweiler, who did such a splendid job on my ragged manuscript, WHITETAIL HUNTING would never have come into being.

I want also to thank my grandfather, Joseph Siciliano, for assisting with the artwork; Betty Jensen, for helping me with the many long hours of typing; my best friend, Sandy Tulli, for the use of his camera; the many hunters that allowed me to examine their deer; all the game management officials and biologists that took the time to answer my numerous questions; William H. Nesbitt, Administrative Director of the Boone and Crockett Club; and Harry E. Hodgdon, Executive Director of The Wildlife Society.

A special thank-you goes to Elizabeth Ralph, who over the many years has allowed me to hunt and study the deer on her land, and to Charles Ralph, for introducing me to this property and taking such good care of it.

Most of all I would like to thank my two little girls, Nikki and Jill, my son, Scott, and my wife, Susan, for their understanding of my love for wildlife and their patience with me during the writing of this book.

Foreword

The whitetail deer is the most hunted big game animal on our continent. They are marvelously adaptive creatures, with an ability to learn quickly as well as to cohabit. They are keen of hearing, sight, and smell. They are quick. They are agile, able to jump a nine-foot fence from a standing position. For their survival they depend on a heightened ability to elude and outwit their enemies, man included, which the statistic that the majority of whitetail are taken within 100 yards or so of the hunter would seem to verify.

The whitetail loves thick brush and frequents the more rolling and forested areas rather than the high altitudes preferred by his cousin the mule deer.

He is not much of a traveler either. In fact, some whitetail live out their entire lifetime in an area as small as a square mile . . .

But they are hard to find.

The whitetail crawls, ducks, sneaks low to the ground, doubles back, makes circles, and lies low. These hide-and-go-seek methods of eluding the hunter mean that anyone who wishes to track and shoot this crafty animal (whether with rifle, bow, or camera) has a formidable task ahead of him.

In writing this book I have tried to cover not only the basic nuts and bolts of whitetail hunting, but also to present some strategies and tips that I have developed myself, and that are new, to help both the beginner and expert gain more satisfaction in his (or her) pursuit of this wonderful, mighty, and clever creature.

1

History and Distribution

The white-tailed deer (*Odocoileus virginianus*) has managed to survive for over 15 million years in spite of man and other predators. Almost 13 million whitetails are alive today. There was a time, though, when it was feared these ruminant (cud-chewer) ungulates (hoofed quadrupeds) wouldn't survive in North America: the late 1800s . . .

When European settlers arrived in North America, there was an abundance of deer—perhaps as many then as there are today. Unfortunately, a shortage of meat and leather in England and Europe gave birth to intensive hunting of deer by professional hunters. In 1646 Rhode Island realized extinction was imminent and passed the first law to protect whitetails. Even though other laws followed, they did little good. At that time people believed that this wonderful natural and renewable resource could not be depleted. The slaughter continued until the late 1800s. At that time the whitetail was nearly extinct in the northeast and dwindling in the rest of the country.

At the turn of the century it was apparent to many states that if they wanted to restore the whitetail herds, they must do a better job of conservation. New laws were passed, and many critical areas such as my home state of New Jersey (which at one time had fewer than 200 whitetails) decided to help things along by importing deer from other states with much larger populations.

Today, man's conservation efforts and the whitetail's unique ability to cohabit with man have brought whitetail numbers to an all-time high. If we leave them enough habitat and continue sound management, these magnificent animals should be around for another 15 million years.

DISTRIBUTION

There are 17 subspecies of the whitetail deer in the United States and Canada and another 13 subspecies below the United States border. Whitetails live in Mexico, Guyana, Bolivia, and Peru. Some species have been introduced into New Zealand, Finland, and Czechoslovakia, and are reportedly doing just fine, especially in New Zealand.

The northern subspecies are larger and darker than the southern subspecies. In the south the deer tend to be smaller and have longer extremities (tails, legs, ears). However, some southern states have imported the northern subspecies to enhance their herd as did many other states during the early 1900s, so classification by geographic location is not exact. For example, New Jersey deer were originally classified as *Odocoileus virginianus borealis*. However, in the early 1900s New Jersey imported both *O.v. borealis and O.v. virginianus*. Yet New Jersey whitetails are usually classified as *O.v. borealis*.

The following list of the seventeen subspecies found north of the Mexican border gives their distinguishing characteristics and distribution.

1. *Odocoileus virginianus borealis*. This is the deer of the northeast woodlands and is the largest and darkest of whitetails. The average adult buck stands 38–41 inches at the shoulder, weighs less than 160 pounds, and may exceed 68 inches in length. However, specimens weighing more than 500 pounds and standing about 51 inches at the shoulder (withers) have been recorded. This subspecies holds the world record rack (antler classification) in the Boone and Crocket Club.

The *borealis* subspecies has the widest range so it is the most hunted of the species. Its territory and numbers are steadily expanding and pushing northward due to increased logging and decreased predation. *O.v. borealis* can be found in Maine, New Hampshire, Vermont, Massachusetts, Connecticut, Rhode Island, New York, New Jersey, Pennsylvania, Maryland, Delaware, Ohio, Indiana, Illinois, Minnesota, Michigan, Wisconsin, Ontario, Quebec, New Brunswick, Nova Scotia, and southeastern Manitoba. At this point I would like to mention that wildlife biologist and provincial deer manager Herb Goulden of the Manitoba Department of Natural Resources indicates that the whitetails in Manitoba are classified as *O.v. manitobensis*. At present I have not been able to locate additional information to support this subspecies classification.

2. *O.v. dacotenis*. Known as the Dakota whitetail, members of this subspecies are about as large as *borealis* in weight and because they have heavy and broad antlers have yielded more high-ranking trophy heads than *borealis*. To study or hunt this elusive animal you must go to North Dakota, South Dakota, Montana, Kansas, Nebraska, Wyoming, Alberta, Saskatchewan, or Manitoba.

3. *O.v. virginianus*. The Virginia whitetail is a fairly large deer with moderately heavy antlers. This adaptable creature inhabits the swamps, coastal marshes, and mountains of Virginia, West Virginia, Tennessee, Kentucky, North and South Carolina, Georgia, Mississippi, and Alabama.

4. *O.v. ochrourus*. Called the Northwest whitetail, this is a large deer with broad antlers. His winter coat is a pale cinnamon-brown and he inhabits parts of Washington, Oregon, Nevada, Idaho, Montana, British Columbia, and Alberta. California reports that they now have only random sightings in the northeast section of the state. Although this subspecies was once known to inhabit the northcentral area of Utah, that state's Division of Natural Resources and Energy-Wildlife Resources returned my questionnaire stating that there are ''NO wild animals in Utah.''

5. *O.v. macrourus*. The Kansas whitetail supports heavy antler beams with short tines and has several trophy heads among the top 25. It inhabits Kansas, Nebraska, Iowa, Oklahoma, Missouri, Arkansas, Louisiana and Texas.

6. *O.v. texanus*. The Texas whitetail, although smaller than its northern cousins, is the largest of the southern deer. The bucks' wide-spreading but thin antlers have several places in the top 25 of the Boone and Crockett Club. The home range for this deer is western Texas, Oklahoma, Kansas, Colorado, New Mexico, and Mexico.

7. *O.v. couesi*. Known as the Arizona whitetail or Coues (cows)

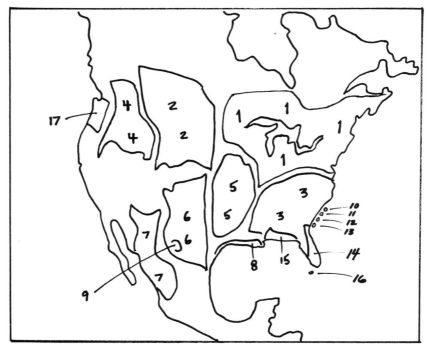

SUBSPECIES DISTRIBUTION (numbers refer to numbers in text)

deer, adults of this subspecies stand about 31 inches high at the shoulder and weigh about 98 pounds. Coues deer have light antlers, and because this was once believed to be a separate species it was given a separate classification in the Boone and Crockett Club. The Coues deer can be found in Arizona's Madrean evergreen woodlands and at the upper limits of the semidesert grasslands of southwestern New Mexico and northern Mexico. Although this subspecies is showing signs of decreased population because of drought and livestock overgrazing during the past few years, their numbers are expected to remain stable with the aid of sound management. Arizona claims to support about 20,000 of the Coues deer, New Mexico reports 10,250, and although Mexico hasn't reported I would suspect the species is doing well there also. Although California once had a population of Coues deer, today they report that there are none to be found in their state.

    8. *O.v. meilhennyi*. The Avery Island whitetail is about the size

of the *texanus* and wears a brownish winter coat. Although its range is limited to the Louisiana and Texas Gulf coast, it integrades with other subspecies.

9. *O.v. carminis*. The Carmen Mountain whitetail is another small deer. Found only in the Carmen Mountains, this little deer is seldom hunted because most of its range lies within Big Bend National Park, Texas. I have no information on Mexican populations.

10. *O.v. taurinsulae*. The Bull's Island whitetail is a medium-sized deer with fairly small antlers with heavy ridges at the base. He is only found on Bull's Island, South Carolina.

11. *O.v. venatorius*. The Hunting Islands whitetail has the same characteristics as the Bull's Island whitetail but can be found only on Hunting Island, South Carolina.

12. *O.v. hiltonensis*. The Hilton Head whitetail is yet another deer with the same physical characteristics as the Bull's Island white-tail. It too has a limited range, and can be found only on Hilton Head Island, South Carolina.

13. *O.v. nigribarbis*. The Blackbeard Island whitetail has the physical appearance of the three South Carolina island subspecies but lives on Blackbeard and Sapelo islands, Georgia.

14. *O.v. seminolus*. The Florida whitetail is about the same size as the Virginia whitetail. Since its habitat includes the wetlands of Georgia and Florida, some call it the deer of the Everglades.

15. *O.v. osceola*. Known as the Florida coastal deer, members of this subspecies are smaller than both the Florida and Virginia white-tails and intergrade with both. The subspecies' range includes the Florida panhandle, southern Alabama, and Mississippi.

16. *O.v. clavium*. The Florida Key deer stands only 26–28 inches high at the shoulder and weighs an average of 45 pounds. In 1949 the Key deer population was at an alltime low of 30. Today, strictly protected, they exceed 300 in number, but are far from being out of danger.

17. *O.v. leucurus*. The Columbian whitetail is also on the endangered species list. Although it once ranged along the Pacific coast of Washington and Oregon, it is now found almost exclusively on the Federal Columbian Whitetailed Deer Refuge near Cathlamet, Washington, where its population is just over 500.

2

Physical Characteristics

Anyone seriously interested in consistently locating deer and predicting their behavior must first of all study, even if only to a minimal degree, their external glands. Because deer are scent-oriented creatures, their scent glands directly regulate their behavior. When I realized this, during my earlier years of studying this unique animal, I increased my enjoyment in the field as well as my hunting success.

Besides the obvious glandular areas of the forehead and tail (antlers and reproductive organs), all deer have four sets of external glands: the interdigital, preorbital, tarsal, and metatarsal.

The interdigital glands (located under the skin between the two hoof lobes) are important to the deer from birth. The strong odor from the waxy secretion of these sudoriferous (sweat-producing) glands stays on the hair around the glands, and is left behind with each step.

It appears that each deer has its own scent because a doe never tracks down a fawn other than her own. The odor produced by the interdigital gland not only helps the deer track one another, it also helps canine predators locate them. However, since once on the trail the canines can also pick up the scents of other deer and cannot tell the difference between the various sets of deer scents, the leaving of a scent trail is of little importance once the chase has begun. Deer will use this flaw in the canines' scenting ability as a way to make an escape. This evasive tactic will be illustrated later when we discuss deer and dogs. The scent left behind by the interdigital glands is the one that the buck in rut follows as he walks through the woods with his tail raised and his nose only a few inches from the ground in search of an estrous doe. A buck in this state of mind is extremely vulnerable. Although buck are always cautious when on a scent trail, the hunter can sometimes make noise and not be detected. On a few occasions while observing bucks thus occupied I have made such goofs as losing my balance while turning around in my tree stand. My noise and movement went practically unnoticed and the bucks quickly resumed their tracking.

The preorbital (lacrymal) glands are the small, trench-like slit of nearly bare skin in front of each eye. They are dark blue or black. The sebaceous (fat-secreting) and sudoriferous glands located here produce an odorous substance called a pheromone, which is released through the hair follicles. Biologists differ as to this gland's importance as a scent producer, but agree that it is basically a sexual stimulant.

Pheromones help cause a very noticeable ritual during the rut. From time to time as a buck trails a doe, or browses through his area, or is making (or has just made) a scrape, he will stop and gently rub the preorbital glands against the tips of branches. When he does this his full attention is given to this delicate procedure, and he gives the hunter time to maneuver or make a well-placed shot at a stationary target.

The most recognizable and probably most familiar glands are the tarsal glands. The tarsal glands are found in the large hairy areas— about three inches across—on the insides of the hind legs at the hock. These glands also produce pheromones but are primarily depositories for urine. Deer spray their urine on the tarsal glands by standing knock-kneed. They often rub the glands together, then lick the tufts after urinating on them. They also often check one another out by smelling and licking these glands. During the rut, this urinating ritual takes place each time a buck makes a scrape or visits a previous scrape. The tarsal glands seem larger, or more noticeable, on the more dominant deer. The tarsal gland seems also to have another purpose: When the deer is alarmed the hairs stand out (flare). This unique phenomenon can be observed.

The metatarsal glands, located between the hocks and the hooves, are probably the least understood of the glands. The metatarsal is not a true gland because it lacks openings or ducts. Biologists believe that the minimal scent the metatarsals produce is deposited on the ground when deer lie down. There seems to be no clear indication of this scent's purpose, but as with the tarsal glands, more dominant deer appear to have larger glands.

For the hunter and researcher the metatarsal gland serves one purpose: identification. The tufts of hair on the metatarsals of whitetails are considerably smaller (about one inch long) than those of the black-tail (2–3 inches) or mule deer (about 5 inches long).

SENSES

Of the five senses—smell, sight, hearing, taste, and touch—by far the most important to the deer is smell. We humans can only marvel at the great powers of smell animals such as deer and dogs have. Our epithelium (which contains mucus membranes and sensory nerve end-

Alerted deer, well aware that something is not right, will cock a leg, ready to stamp it. Also, their ears become erect and move forward, and the hair over their tarsal glands flares, as a warning to other deer.

Being well camouflaged means little if the deer can pick up your scent, as this deer has.

ings which are in turn connected to the olfactory bulbs) has a skin surface area relatively much less than that of a dog's epithelium. A dog has 10 times the ability of a human to smell any scent. Although no one is exactly sure how much epithelium surface area is involved with deer, many biologists believe that the scenting capability of deer is near that of dogs.

I believe that the deer's sense of smell is considerably *greater* than that of a dog. I say this because I have yet to see a dog, domestic or wild, become aware of my presence in the woods (when I am being careful) at a distance greater than 10 yards, whereas deer have scented me at distances greater than two hundred yards on several occasions.

However, this wonderfully powerful sense is dependent upon several variables. Wind can greatly reduce the power of smell. Scents can be carried in a straight line (warning deer); they can be scattered about in swirls and air pockets (alarming and confusing them); or they can be carried away (giving no warning whatever).

Temperature too determines the effectiveness of the deer's sense of smell. Higher temperatures cause the air to rise and carry scents upward. The hotter the day, the faster the process. Cold air of course carries scents downward.

Humidity is another factor which affects whitetails' powers of smell. As a rule, high humidity is ideal for scenting because the deer's nasal membranes are moist and extremely receptive. However, too humid conditions—such as fog and mist—tend to slow the rate at which scents travel from source to nose. Rain or snow push the scent down to the ground and destroy it. Low humidity—below 25 percent— also works against the sense of smell because it dries out deer's nasal membranes. Dry nasal membranes cannot pick up scent. If you watch deer on a day with low humidity you will see them flick their tongues against their noses from time to time to moisten the membranes.

Deer use their sense of smell not only to locate danger and each other, but also to locate food. They can find acorns, for instance, under snow and piles of leaves with their sensitive noses.

Hearing is probably the whitetail's second most important defense system. The long, cup-shaped ears are constantly in motion and often act independently. They swivel around to pick up the slightest sound, no matter how faint it may be. Many times the snap of a twig or the rustle of some leaves will put an end to a long and well-planned stalk.

With their sharp hearing, deer can differentiate among sounds. For instance, a squirrel jumping through leaves seems to get little more than a twitch of an ear and/or a fast glance . . . yet the nearly silent approach of a deer from a different herd will often draw considerable attention. Sounds which have become familiar, such as the chainsaw, are merely an annoyance: the deer won't expose themselves but they usually won't leave the area either (unless approached). Many times while bowhunting I've watched deer bed down within 100 yards of a man cutting wood with a chainsaw. They react to automobiles in the same way. On several occasions I have seen both buck and doe bed down just yards from a well-used road.

Sounds that deer can hear but not identify provoke a different reaction. Usually they become both curious and cautious—almost without fail they will want to investigate. In such an instance the ears are poised at near right angles to the head or sometimes straight up and cupped in the direction of the noise. The deer advance, stiff-legged, with their necks stretched out but lowered nearly level with their backs.

Their heads will pop up and down, and if worried they will circle or stamp their feet (to provoke movement from the noise source), snorting if spooked enough. If there is no response from the source of the noise and they cannot smell anything suspect, they will usually relax a bit and resume their business.

Whitetails' curiosity about noise has put meat on the table more than once for me. Several years ago I was trying to get close to a herd of deer but the leaves were too dry for a successful stalk. I knew where the deer were headed and it was out of my territory, so I tied one end of a thin nylon rope to a thick bush. After hiding, some 25 feet away, I began to shake the bush—just loudly enough to catch their attention. After a few minutes, a few of them cautiously advanced. Fifteen minutes later I filled my tag.

Sight, I sometimes believe, is the whitetail's poorest sense. It seems that their eyes detect only motion and not image. I've been caught out in the open several times with nothing to hide behind except my gun or bow, and did not spook the deer merely because I didn't move. It just seems that they don't recognize a man unless they scent him or see him move. This is not to imply that if you don't move you won't eventually be spotted, for I am convinced beyond a doubt that deer know their area extremely well and will notice anything new. For instance, one summer while spotting deer and preparing to try out some new deer scents, I knocked over an old rotted tree about eight inches in diameter. It fell across an abandoned jeep path by a deer run. Later, two does came bounding out of the woods toward a field. When they saw the tree they stopped for about four seconds. It was no danger to them, but it hadn't been there before and they knew it. If it had been a man, they would have had the edge on him.

To understand why movement, rather than image, is noticed by the deer, one must understand the physical characteristics of the white-tail's eyes. First, their eyes are on the sides of their skulls, which increases their ability to see behind them. With the curvature of the eyes they can view at least 300 degrees of their surroundings in mon-ocular vision (each eye viewing independently of the other) and about 50 degrees in binocular vision (having the use of both eyes to view an object).

Deer see horizontal patterns better than vertical ones. Camouflage suits and camouflage makeup are therefore advantageous if applied in a vertical pattern, if the surrounding cover is not horizontal (such as pine tree branches).

The retinae of deer's eyes have very few cones (which are responsible for color reception). In fact, their retinae are almost entirely composed of rods, which register light intensity. This explains why the whitetail, as well as other deer, does not see color. They cannot see the full spectrum, merely shades of light and dark. They are able to see at night, since rods reflect light.

Deer also have the ability to increase their dimensional perception by moving their head from side to side. And this of course is one more reason to remain still when deer are looking in your general direction.

Taste is another deer sense the hunter or naturalist should consider. Like humans, deer prefer sweet foods—white acorns instead of black for instance. They also prefer browse with higher moisture content (live leaves over dry dead leaves). They also like to eat tender young shoots rather than thicker, tougher branches (see *Food Preferences and Patterns*). Contrary to common belief, however, whitetails will try foods that are not native to their habitat. In my area many people have purchased exotic plants for their yards and have found that, much to their dismay, the deer find them quite tasty.

Touch is a sense that researchers are just beginning to explore in detail. For the hunter, sexual touching—such as the buck and doe rubbing, sniffing, and licking during mating—is of great interest.

I am sure that deer possess a "sixth sense" that tells them when danger is imminent even though no physical signals have been received. On several occasions I have had all the advantages a hunter could ask for: the wind in my face, an overcast day with no shadows, the deer coming in from a direction opposite that which I traveled to reach my stand, and good cover in my tree stand. Yet, as I waited at full draw, the deer stopped, hunched up, and ran from the area for no apparent reason other than a sudden fear.

Their sixth sense also seems to tell them when a storm is about to hit. On numerous occasions the sky would be nearly cloudless as I entered the woods before dawn. Looking at the beautiful twinkling stars on a cool morning would really start my day off right. Once settled in the woods though, I would find deer browsing at an unusually high rate . . . and without fail the temperature would drop more than 20 degrees and the sky would dump a few inches of snow.

In warmer weather this high browsing activity usually means a hard rain lasting more than a day.

I wish the weather forecasting people were as accurate as the deer!

ANTLERS

The antler pedicles (the bony extensions of the frontal bone from which the antlers will be formed) can be felt when the young buck is about 2 or 3 months old, and are visible at the age of 6 months. At this point these circular protuberances are often called "buttons." However, the buck's first set of antlers usually won't break through the skin covering of the pedicles until the deer reaches the age of about 10 months. I say *usually* because on several occasions I have found yearlings with small polished spikes of up to 2 inches long instead of the expected "buttons."

In my home state of New Jersey, the antler development begins in early April. In spring, lengthening daylight hours—the photoperiod—stimulate the pituitary gland, which produces a somatotropic hormone, which governs tissue growth. Blood vessels deposit bone salts on the pedicle. As the antlers grow, a velvet-like skin covering encases the soft, fast-growing bone tissue. About ½ inch of antler growth per day is possible during the early stages of development. By the end of May the first fork will usually appear.

If a buck grows a typical rack, the main beams will project backward from the pedicle until they are long enough to reach between the ears. At that point they start to curve upward and outward, then to the sides, forward, and slightly inward again, almost as if they were trying to encircle an object, such as a tree.

On the main beams will be points or tines. The tines nearest the pedicle are called browtines or eyeguards. The second set of tines on the mainbeams are usually the longest on the rack. As additional tines emerge along the beams, they become progressively shorter in length. The ends of the beams are also classified as tines.

Antler racks are classified as "non-typical" if the tines are not symmetrical. Non-typical racks have their own classification for the

Gail Ann Eisnitz

record books and generally have many more points than a "typical" rack.

If the food supply is good, and the buck remains free from injury and sickness, then his antlers may eventually resemble his father's. I say this because it has been found that heredity is connected to antler growth.

By July most of the points (tines) have been formed, the antlers' maximum width (spread) has been obtained, and the calcification process, which will eventually turn the antlers to bone, has begun to take place at the base of the antlers.

In August, as the rut nears, the testicles become active. They enlarge and descend from the body. The scrotum will also enlarge and become visible. As the male hormone testosterone is produced, the antlers stop growing and the blood flow to them is shut off. The antlers will no longer be masses of connective tissue produced by the dermis (second layer of skin); they will now become impregnated with lime.

During September the testosterone level rises markedly. The testes

Buck rubbing his antlers. *Photo by Leonard Lee Rue III.*

form sperm and the buck is now capable of reproducing. The sharp increase of testosterone causes the buck's neck to swell and also completes the hardening of the antlers. Once the antlers are fully hardened the buck quickly removes their velvet covering. This is usually done in one day with the aid of a convenient sapling.

From my observations of bucks rubbing, it seems that the first rubbing, although sometimes rapid, is not nearly as aggressive as those that take place nearer the rut.

The buck does a very thorough job of removing the velvet from his antlers. He picks a sturdy but forgiving sapling and rubs his antlers lengthwise along the trunk. He rubs between the tines and on the inside and outside of the antlers' curve. To get the velvet off the antler base, he turns his head sideways—parallel to the ground.

Rubbing seems to excite the buck highly. The more he rubs the faster he goes and the more pressure he applies to the sapling. The blood residue of the velvet will often stain the polished antlers.

It has been found that the biggest, strongest bucks are the ones to peel first. Bucks have a favorite rubbing tree in a preferred area. It doesn't take a buck long to scar several saplings and brush in his area, so don't think that a lot of rubs mean a lot of bucks. If you find some rubs while scouting an area, look for paths to other rubs. You can use these rubs as indications of the extent of a buck's range. However, you must remember that a rub is usually used only once. It would be a waste of time to take a stand for the purpose of waiting for a buck to return to a rub.

While checking out rubs, note the size of the hoofprints and the saplings used: very often, but not always, big bucks use big saplings, and make big rubbed areas.

As the weather cools, whitetail bucks become more aggressive. The swelling of the neck becomes more noticeable. They become ready for mating weeks before the doe does and, because the does won't accept the males yet, their frustration mounts. Bucks attack saplings with all their strength, preparing for confrontations with other bucks. As the rut advances, their attacks become even fiercer, and their movements are almost a blur as they subdue their imaginary rivals.

At this time bucks advertise their presence by making scrapes. They travel constantly to locate does that will accept them. During these few weeks, before the does are ready, a hunter stands the best chance of taking a buck.

Although the bigger bucks will usually select a bigger tree or sapling and make a larger rub area, you can't depend on the size of the rub to determine the size of the deer. Both of these rubs were made by one buck. The size of the hoofprints near the base of the rub is a truer indication of the size of the deer.

Buck on the trail of a doe. Note raised tail and ears laid back showing aggression. *Photo by Leonard Lee Rue III.*

THE RUTTING RITUAL

Observing and understanding the mysterious rutting ritual makes hunting more pleasurable and considerably increases your chances of success.

One of the unique rituals I see each year is the "hide and seek" game. As the buck searches for a receptive doe he holds his tail out and keeps his nose near the ground as he tries to pick up a scent. If he finds a doe (be she ready or not) he will stretch his neck out and head rapidly toward her. If the doe is not yet ready she will not let a mature buck get near her. However, younger bucks are sometimes tolerated, though not accepted as breeding partners.

On more than one occasion I have seen a buck head into a large thicket to start a little romance—and the does run through the thicket to avoid him. Sometimes, if a buck persists, the does will split up and disperse. Not knowing which one to follow the would-be suiter gives up and heads back toward one of his scrapes to pick up another scent.

Once in a while does will urinate while running. A buck smells the urine, raises his head, and curls his upper lip. This concentrates the urine odor at his nostrils and he can immediately tell if the doe is in estrus. If the doe is not in estrus the buck will leave and continue his search. Bucks in this condition attempt to sniff the genitals and hocks of every doe they encounter.

A doe actively seeks a buck about two days before she comes into estrus. At this time her vulva swells and she urinates on her tarsal glands frequently. Even though she may be ready for mating, she may not let a buck mount her right away. They caress each other by licking and rubbing their bodies for stimulation. Actual congress is very short. After mounting the doe, the buck makes only a couple of short thrusts and then with a hard lunge ejaculates and withdraws immediately. The thrust may be powerful enough to knock the doe onto her knees.

Immediately after the mating the doe squats, as if she wished to urinate, or stands with her back humped.

Once a buck finds a doe coming into estrus, he stays with her the day before she actually comes into estrus, then spends a day copulating

Buck scenting a doe. Note curled lip. *Photo by Leonard Lee Rue III.*

with her. Once the doe has conceived, she loses interest in the buck and the two go their separate ways.

The buck continues his search for receptive does.

A buck often breeds a doe several times before traveling on to find another. With luck he may mate as many as 20 does during the 60 days of the rut—and if there is ample food the rut may be longer.

As the buck travels to find more does he gets into fights with bucks from other herds and sometimes even with bucks from his own herd. When two bucks with overlapping territories meet during the rut a battle nearly always takes place.

One or both bucks will lower their hindquarters slightly and lay their ears back. The aggressor will extend his neck and lower his head so that it is lower than his back. With his rack extended forward and his tail tucked down he is ready to meet his foe. Even at a distance you can see the hair along his back stand up.

He stands for a few minutes in a tense, hunched position, as if showing off his muscles. He flicks his tongue in and out, licking his nose.

With stiff legs the bucks approach each other in a sidling fashion and circle each other like two boxers in a ring. They make grunts that can be heard over 100 yards away. When they are within 20 feet of each other, they lunge at each other with great force.

Bucks battling during the rut. *Photo by Leonard Lee Rue III.*

Sometimes this charge will break their antlers or lock them together, which will mean death by starvation for both deer. Fortunately, antler locking is rare. Usually the battle becomes a pushing and shoving match, lasting 5–30 minutes and ending when contact is broken and one buck retreats. I say *usually* because I have seem two bucks fight on and off for a period of 50 minutes. Although they were nearly the same size, the slightly heavier buck eventually prevailed.

SCRAPE HUNTING

Of the many "signs" made by whitetail bucks, the scrape is the most valuable to the hunter. It is proof that at least one buck inhabits the immediate area and is likely to return in the near future.

Most hunters do not properly read and understand scrapes. They see a scrape as a guarantee of success. A novice hunter will often stand near any kind of scrape and wait for a buck to come walking carelessly along—but unless he has taken the time to analyze the scrape, the hunter can really waste a lot of his time. In fact, he may be better off just watching a trail.

Scrape hunting is a science and requires a lot of work and time, especially if you wish to identify and take the largest buck in your area. If you do your preseason scouting well, scrapes can lead you to a specific buck.

To use scrapes effectively, a hunter should first know how and why they are made. Scrapes are roughly-circular areas of earth that bucks make by pawing at the ground with their hooves (not their antlers, as some may believe) to expose the moist soil beneath the surface. Because scrapes are usually made in a frenzied manner, they are easily seen from a distance in the forest.

The size of the scrape depends on the kind of scrape being made, the number of deer using it (more than one buck often uses a scrape), the frequency of its use (most active as the rut nears), and the kind of soil (clay stays moist longer than sand).

Almost without fail, scrapes will be located under overhanging branches. These branches are usually 4–5 feet above the scrape, so that the buck can reach up and hook them with his antlers. He does this very vigorously and leaves the branches quite mangled. He leaves his scent on them by rubbing his peorbital glands against them. From time to time he may chew some branches, then continue to make his scrape.

Once the pawing is completed, the buck may defecate or urinate in the scrape. When he does this he sprays urine on the tarsal glands inside his hind legs at the joint or hock. To urinate on his tarsal glands he supports most of his weight on his front feet and twists his hind legs inward so that he appears knock-kneed. While urinating he rubs his tarsal glands against each other. The more dominant a buck is in his area, the more he urinates on his tarsal glands.

Once finished urinating, he steps all over the scrape—or at least puts one foot in it, leaving another scent with his interdigital glands (between the lobes of each hoof). This scent is left behind each time he puts his hoof down.

If another deer approaches the area, the buck will check to see if it is a doe. He puts his nose close to the ground and extends his tail while following the new scent to its source.

A doe in estrus will stay in the area of the scrape and even seek out the buck aggressively.

Young bucks make scrapes different from those made by older and more mature bucks. They also make more of them. Because there

Buck rubbing and urinating on his tarsal glands. *Photo by Leonard Lee Rue III.*

Notice the faint hoofprints left behind in the scrape made by both buck and visiting doe.

are different kinds of scrapes, it is important to be aware of the differences among them and understand what they mean.

Scrape hunting and interpretation is a science.

Territory scrapes. This title is a bit misleading because bucks don't have a territory in the usual sense. They have dispersal areas that generally overlap at least the area of one other buck. The territory scrape is therefore only an indication that a buck is in the area.

Territory scrapes are numerous and are made soon after a buck sheds his velvet. They are usually made by yearling bucks under cover of darkness. They are usually elongated instead of oval or round.

Although made at random in the young buck's home area, most are located along the edges of thickets or streams and between wooded sections and fields. Once made they are forgotten. If you take the time to follow a path from one scrape to another, you will locate a buck's primary domain. As he grows older, and expands his territory, he will still spend most of his time in this area and make his scrapes in similar terrain.

Territory scrape . . . note the elongated quality of the scrape–instead of oval or round. This scrape was not used or revisited by either buck or doe. Although made under an overhanging branch, this long-shaped scrape is a typical territory scrape, merely showing a buck's presence.

Closeup of territory scrape.

Secondary scrapes.   As the rut nears, a different type of scrape appears. The purpose of this scrape is to let the doe know that a buck is available for mating. More mature bucks make this kind of scrape. This scrape measures 2–3 feet across and may be a few inches deep. It is usually made on or near a well-used trail or even an unused dirt road or fire cut. Unfortunately for the hunter, the buck which makes the scrape usually visits it only at night and only once or twice a week. Therefore, it would behoove the hunter to locate his stand in an area containing several scrapes, especially during the early season and early in the rut.

After a rain, bucks frantically revisit all their scrapes to renew them. Because these visits are usually made at night, the hunter should take his stand very early in the morning to catch a buck making his rounds.

If a secondary scrape appears to be unused for a while, it may be because the buck has been spooked from the area or because he has taken up with a doe that has come into early estrus. If after a few days the scrape is not renewed, head for another.

Secondary scrape . . . note that the scrape is rounded and under overhanging branches. The 29-inch arrow lying on the ground beside the scrape shows that the scrape is over two feet in diameter.

Aside from locating bucks, secondary scrapes are valuable because they indicate the peak of the rut. By watching several scrapes at the same time, a hunter can tell when rutting activity picks up. It will be apparent in all areas at the same time. It lasts for only a few days and then there is a sudden slowing of scrape activity. At this point the peak of the rut is less than one month away, if the weather remains normal for the area. If the weather suddenly becomes cold, the rut comes sooner; if it turns warm, the rut is delayed.

Primary Scrapes.   A primary scrape is usually at least three feet across and, if the ground is soft, a few inches deep. Once you have seen a primary scrape you will have no trouble identifying it.

Primary scrapes are opened when the secondary scrapes dwindle in activity. If you are familiar with all the older secondary scrapes in your area, a brand new one will be a primary scrape.

The best thing about primary scrapes is that they appear year after year in the same area. This is because the primary scrape is a breeding area. Unless encroachment or a severe food crisis occurs, a primary scrape will usually be used year after year (if its maker survives the wintering season). Even if he doesn't . . . I have sometimes seen a scrape used by a new buck during the following season. So once you find one, remember where it is.

In farm areas I often find primary scrapes less than 100 yards from a main feeding area. Very often there will be many secondary and primary scrapes near each other. Heavy brush areas around secondary scrapes may contain a primary scrape. If you can't find one during the season, you may be able to find one in the early spring because there will probably be no leaves in that area.

It is important for any hunter who wants to take a large buck to pass up the small bucks which come to a scrape. The big ones tend to shy away from a scrape when the smaller ones show up at them. Larger bucks don't like to expose themselves when smaller bucks are about. They stay in the nearby brush and keep tabs on the scrape by scent. By staying downwind, a buck can catch the scent of any estrous doe approaching the scrape and not expose himself unless absolutely necessary. If you decide to take a stand near a primary scrape, approach the area with caution and be constantly aware of the wind. If spooked, a buck may not come back to that scrape for several days.

Primary scrape . . . note the size of this scrape. Several bucks will visit and probably breed near this site. This is the fourth year in a row that this particular spot has been used for a primary scrape location. Each year it was initiated by different bucks.

Deer inhabiting forests are more active than farmland deer. Because of the size of the area and relative scarcity of food, does must travel more to find food. Their extensive travels make it necessary for the buck to keep freshening and checking his scrapes in case one of the traveling does wanders into his area. In reality, an estrous doe will make the needed effort to find a buck for herself—yet the buck continues to maintain his scrapes diligently, as if they were his only key to finding a mate.

An observer can tell a day or two ahead of time when a doe is in estrus. Her daytime activities increase at least twofold and her nighttime activities several times. Within two days after copulation, her activity abruptly declines.

In farm areas, the abundance of food and cover reduces the need for travel. Does are ever-present. This ensures that farmland bucks will mate more often than their cousins in the forest.

Anyone wishing to hunt at scrapes must have patience and should not give up on a scrape as long as it is being used. Sooner or later a large buck will appear.

ANTLER SHEDDINGS

After breeding, there is a sharp drop in the testosterone level. This, combined with a shortened photoperiod (which causes the pituitary to slow down activity), causes shedding of the antlers at the pedicle. Scientists are also considering the possibility that a sudden drop in androgen—another male hormone—after the rut may cause the antlers to be shed. The exact relationship between these occurrences has not been determined.

Many observers, myself included, have noted that the larger bucks shed their antlers earlier than the younger, less sexually active bucks. Perhaps this is because of their higher breeding activity and greater use of testosterone.

Recent shedding of an antler. *(Photo by Leonard Lee Rue III)*

Although shedding often begins as early as late December in some parts of the country, it can last up until April in others. Coues deer may shed as late as June. This lengthy shedding period may reflect an abundance of high quality browse, which extends the breeding season.

THE STOMACH

There is one more organ of the deer that must be mentioned in this section, because it is a key to their survival: the stomach.

As I mentioned earlier, deer are ruminants, cud-chewing animals with four-chambered stomachs. This kind of stomach enables deer to gather and swallow great quantities of food in a short time. Then, while they are relaxing in a safe place, it can be chewed at their leisure. On the surface this sounds like a great asset, and it is—to a point . . . but there's a catch . . .

While feeding, a deer concentrates on locating and obtaining food. To do this the deer must use its eyes and nose, use them, that is, exclusively for the purpose of food gathering, thus reducing awareness of predators and other dangers. The deer's hearing is impaired as well, because as its jaws crush the leaves and twigs it is eating the noise is transmitted through the auditory system.

Thus, because they become so engrossed in the feeding process that their senses are slightly impaired, feeding deer must keep on the move. They will never spend very much time feeding in one spot, thus preventing any predator from getting too close to them. The greater the distance between them and a predator, the less the predator's chances of remaining undetected while approaching.

Also, of course, feeding deer invariably face into the wind, which will carry potentially dangerous scents to them as they feed.

3

Food Preferences And Patterns

Deer will browse on just about anything. However, like people, they have foods they prefer. As the seasons change so does their preference.

The acorn is probably the whitetail's single most preferred wild food. They are highly digestable and contain a large amount of crude fat. Crude fat content is an index of the potential energy of a food. In other words, deer will acquire and store weight at a rapid rate by eating acorns.

To deer and other wildlife the real appeal of acorns is related to their palatability and seasonal abundance. Some acorns are available for long periods during autumn and winter, when other fleshy fruits degrade. Black oak acorns, although higher in digestible energy, have a high tannin content and are therefore less palatable than the sweeter white oak acorns. However, they remain available longer because white acorns germinate soon after falling—something worth remembering by the late season hunter or wildlife observer.

Acorns are also a delight to the farmer, since deer prefer them to crops (corn excluded). Although whitetails will consume large quantities of acorns, they must continue to move as they browse. This means they must have other favorite foods to head for.

One of those favorites in the beech tree. I have often seen deer prefer beech leaves to acorns in the late season. Hickory nuts and pecans are also actively sought . . . but walnuts are not. Even squirrels don't bother too much with them.

If you are unfamiliar with tree varieties and identification characteristics, just look for squirrels. An abundance of the little creatures indicates the presence of preferred nuts in the area. Watch where they pick up nuts, then check out that area to identify the kind of nuts being collected near the base of the trees.

Ferns are also noticeably preferred browse from fall to spring. During late autumn I have noticed quite a concentration of deer in areas where ferns grow. They will browse on them while heading to and returning from their favorite feeding areas.

Brambles, particularly the timber species, are definitely a favorite browse. Brambles are not only preferred for their food content, but also because they offer deer needed security.

Whitetails prefer different foods at different times of the year.

In summer, green leaves of trees, shrubs, ferns, and brambles are favored. In fall, woody stems are eaten as green leaves decrease. As the leaves fall, deer will prefer freshly fallen, moist leaves over old dry ones. Deer also prefer the sweeter-tasting red leaves to all the rest. Dark leaves such as oak and elm are very seldom chosen early in the fall.

In winter, deer browse will consist primarily of tree and shrub twigs. Dry leaves, green ferns, and grasses are also important items at that time.

When spring arrives deer will feed on the new growth of ferns, grasses, sedges, forbs, and any new shoots they can locate. New shoots are always preferred as browse through the year. Agricultural crops, as any farmer or gardener will point out, are always a favorite food when available. Some of these are corn, clover, apples, pears, soybeans, alfalfa, and pumpkins.

Even eight-foot-high fences cannot keep deer out of the garden. Near where I do most of my hunting there are farms and houses with small gardens, and nearly every garden has a fence around it at least eight feet high . . . but I have seen deer jump over them from a standing position!

4

Recommended Weapons

The whitetail, being a rather small but vivacious animal, is most often killed at close range. Therefore it is not necessary to use large-bore or flat-shooting guns. The 30/30, .32 Special, and .35-caliber bores have cleanly taken millions of deer over the years, and if you are hunting in open or mixed terrain, the 7mm Magnum, .270, and .243 are good choices, along with the popular .30/06 and .308 calibers.

The slugs used should be of the round-nosed, thick-jacket type.

The terrain is usually heavy, and so a wise choice for your whitetail gun is one that is of carbine length and capable of fairly rapid second shots. The lever action is very popular, followed by the pump and, where allowed, the automatic . . . but let's get into this in detail.

SINGLE-SHOT ACTION

Many years ago rifles with single-shot actions, such as rolling-block and falling-block types, were the best around—definitely much faster and more dependable than the muskets they replaced. The Remington rolling block was so well liked throughout the world that it became a standard military rifle. Single shot actions were made in a variety of calibers, from .22 to the big buffalo-hunting favorites, the .38 and .50.

Problems arose when cartridges increased in power due to the use of smokeless powder, which caused extraction problems when the powder was loaded in soft brass cartridges.

Repeating actions solved the problem.

The new repeating actions were a blessing to hunters, who could get off a second or third shot faster than they could reload a single-shot rifle.

Today, even though the action has been greatly improved, the single shot is seldom used except to train novices. For hunting purposes, it would be best to use such light guns in rugged territory on game such as goats or sheep, where the hunter usually gets but one shot.

I have mixed feelings about using single-shot rifles for whitetail hunting. Because of the usually densely-wooded habitat, and the strength and speed of the animals, a fast second shot should be available. However, I also feel that all hunters should start hunting with this type of action for one reason: to learn to make the first shot count.

On numerous occasions I have seen so-called hunters snap-shoot and empty their repeater's magazine in two or three seconds, relying on firepower instead of accuracy. That's OK in the military but not in the woods. Needless to say, in nearly every instance these firepower addicts missed or made poor hits.

LEVER ACTION

For a long time lever-action rifles, such as the famous Winchester Model 94, were the favorite hunting rifle in the country. The lever action is easy to operate, offers a fast second shot, and does not have to be opened in order to load the tubular magazine. The lever action is chambered for light-to-medium-caliber cartridges at moderate pressures, and is therefore ideal for short-range wooded areas.

The side-ejection mechanisms on the newer models make them ideal for mounting scopes.

Lever-action rifles have some shortcomings, though. Because of the tubular magazine you can use only round-nosed bullets, since a pointed bullet would rest on the primer of the cartridge ahead of it in the magazine. A stiff recoil or dropped gun could mean disaster. The extraction of dirty, oversized, or soft cases is also a problem because lever actions lack the strong camming action of a Mauser-type bolt. Also, lever actions do not lock very securely at the breech-bolt, and this allows cartridge cases to stretch when fired. Although this is only a minor flaw, still it is something one might consider when purchasing a new piece of equipment. Newer models will probably have stronger actions.

Even with the minor imperfections mentioned, there is something special about a lever-action rifle. Somehow it feels and handles just right.

PUMP ACTIONS

For whitetail hunting with heavier rifles, this action is ideal, since it is the second-fastest action available, after the semi-automatic. The breechbolt has locks with multiple lugs at the head, but, naturally, does not have the extracting power of a bolt action. The action is smooth and, as you would expect from a pump, works well from the shoulder, so you can keep your eye on the target.

Although it is not as accurate as the bolt or the semi-automatic, the pump-action is more than sufficient for typical whitetail habitat.

SEMI-AUTOMATICS

Gas-operated, semi-automatic rifles are surprisingly accurate, and their action is by far the fastest. However, as I mentioned in the section on the singleshot action, too many inexperienced hunters misuse this speed. Unlike the other actions, the semi-automatic does not force the shooter to slow down and think before he fires a second time. A novice with a semi-automatic will usually spray the area with lead.

For example, about 10 a.m. one recent opening day I was on stand where I knew a nice nine-point buck would be traveling (if he didn't get spooked that is). On schedule, the buck and a friend of his started up from a ravine toward the top of a hill, where I patiently waited with my double-barreled shotgun and #4 buckshot.

Unfortunately, as he got within 90 yards, another hunter on an adjoining property some 70 yards away opened up on him. He fired three shots so fast they sounded like one shot. The pellets knocked branches off trees all around the two deer, but they both immediately turned around and left the area unharmed. Had the man taken his time between shots, he probably would have had one of them.

A discussion later with the hunter who couldn't believe he had missed both deer proved my point. He was inexperienced and, had he nailed one of the deer, it would have been his first.

Firepower failed.

DOUBLE RIFLE

Few hunters have seen a double rifle but most are familiar with the double-barreled shotgun and the over-and-under shotgun. I was among this group until recently, when tracking in the Pennsylvania woods I met a man lugging this heavy piece of iron. A family hierloom given him by his father several years earlier, it was made in England and, though chambered for the .30/06, worked on the same principle as the double shotgun. Thus it offered excellent speed in aiming, a low sight line, and a fast second shot if needed. If one barrel misfires you still have the other to depend on. Accuracy was "marginal at best," the man reported however.

The double gun is practically a collectors item now, and with a price tag of several thousand dollars for a good one, you can see why.

BOLT ACTIONS

Without a doubt, the most popular rifle action in the world today is the bolt action, particularly the Mauser type. It was introduced in 1888 and modified several times before 1898, but since then has undergone only minor changes.

Simply put, the action is a turnbolt type and has two large locking lugs at the front end of the bolt and a locking lug at the root of the bolt. The front locking lugs turn into recesses in the receiver ring and the locking lug at the root also turns into a recess. The box-type magazine can accept pointed cartridges.

The Mauser type is not the only bolt action available, but it is the most imitated and is preferred by both sportsmen and gunsmiths because of its strength and simplicity.

Other actions are the British Short Lee Enfield, the Mannlicher-Schoenauer, and the Krag-Jorgenson, to name a few.

Accuracy, rigidity (to prevent case stretching), excellent camming (to extract fired cartridges), and ease of chambering another cartridge are some of the bolt action's better points. The action is also virtually jam-proof, even in foul weather.

Because of its popularity, the bolt action has the widest variety of chambers and cartridges of all the actions, and if you are one of the many sportsmen who have only one or two rifles, it would be to your advantage to own at least one of this well-liked, dependable type.

CALIBERS

You can get into quite a discussion on this subject and I am sure to get plenty of heat on this, but here goes. Some hunters believe the faster the bullet the less deflection from branches because the fast spinning will keep it on course, much as a spinning top resists deflection when you hit it.

In part, I agree. Speed and spin *will* keep a bullet on course. But should one use a light-weight bullet, there is a limit to what speed and spin can do to make up for lower mass. It is a fact that the heavier the bullet the more energy it takes to deflect it. In other words, a heavy bullet is harder to deflect than a light one—and even harder if it is traveling at a high speed. Also, a heavier bullet will stay together longer when deflected. Fast, light, thin-jacketed bullets (under 100 gr.) seem to disintegrate when they hit one or two branches.

In whitetail hunting, one must keep in mind that the animal seldom weighs over 300 pounds—and usually weighs under 175 pounds on the hoof. Whitetails inhabit thick woodlands and brush areas, and the average killing range is less than 100 yards. Few shots exceed 200 yards, so even the slow .30/30 is acceptable.

Heck, that caliber has killed quite a lot of deer in its day. It is not a favorite of mine, but at under 200 yards in the woods it does a wonderful job.

Since deflection is such a major factor in whitetail hunting it is worth some looking into. I have seen several hunters shoot at deer through more than twenty feet of brush, and the result in most cases was a miss. The infuriated hunters were quick to blame their equipment instead of themselves—human nature I guess. Naturally, shooting through that much brush with a rifle is not a wise thing to do, but it does happen.

Through experimentation, I've developed a "brush-bucking" theory.

I decided to find out just how much various bullets are deflected in thick woods. I fired several rounds (ten each) of .243 caliber, 100 grain soft-points, and .30/06, 180 grain soft-points through some pretty heavy brush at targets up to 25 feet away. As I had suspected, all the light (.243 caliber) bullets performed poorly. At 10 feet the bullets that made it to the target were off by more than 10 inches—a miss or a bad hit on a deer. The .30/06 bullets were off an average of only 6 inches at 10 feet, 12 inches at 15 feet, and at 25 feet all but one missed (over 18 inches off). As you already know, both calibers are fast and hit hard. It was weight that made the vital difference. In the woods competition is stiff and I like to have as much of an advantage as possible.

Although each person has his own thoughts and theories on deer calibers, I would like to list my favorites for whitetail hunting.

For hunters who like to hunt in open fields or along power lines, I recommend a minimum caliber of .243, 100 grain; in the woods, a minimum of .270 Winchester, 130 grain; .30/30 Winchester, 150 grain; .300 Savage, 150 grain; .30/06, 150 or 180 grain; .32 Winchester Special, 170 grain; .35 Remington, 200 grain; or .308, 180 grain.

Most all sporting goods dealers stock these calibers. When you are miles from home and find that your ammunition is bad or has been misplaced, you will quickly realize the benefit of choosing one of the calibers suggested.

BULLET SELECTION

The whitetail is a fairly light animal with a thin skin, light bones, and thin muscles, so penetration is no problem. The ideal bullet, therefore, would be one which opens fast, since experience has shown that bullets which open up too slowly causes superficial damage and often lead to long, difficult tracking or the loss of the deer to another hunter.

On several occasions, while walking through the woods, I have come across a deer's blood trail. All too often the trail will be thin or consist of intermittent spots and pinpoint-sized drops. Then, usually about 100 yards away, I will see a hunter trying to track his deer.

When the hunter gets to my location, I help him track. And eventually we find it, or its guts . . . because some other hunter has gotten to it first.

Of the deer I have helped locate, I have often found that although the hit was OK the bullet went completely through the deer causing minimal damage. The reason? Virtually every one of the hunters had used a controlled-expanding-type bullet (too much jacket). The bullet passed through the deer, making only a small hole—and that, in most cases, too high in the vital area to cause much external bleeding, which of course made for a very poor trail. Controlled-expansion bullets should be used for bear, elk, and moose, not for the light-weight whitetail.

The ideal bullet weighs at least 130 grains, maximizing both momentum and knockdown power. It has a soft lead core, so it will open quickly, a thin jacket to hold the bullet together until impact, and a flat, open, or round nose for resistance to brush deflection.

Some hunters say this kind of bullet tears up too much meat. I have three answers for them: First, the purpose of the bullet is to expand quickly and violently to cause shock and massive hemorrhaging in a vital area for a fast, humane kill. Secondly, there is very little meat, if any, to be destroyed in the vital rib-cage target area. Thirdly, if you miss the vital area and hit the meat section, you will destroy most of that meat no matter what bullet you shoot.

The bottom line is that if you are going to shoot, shoot effectively.

SHOTGUNS FOR WHITETAILS

Under any circumstances shotguns are ideal weapons for whitetail hunting. In fact, in some areas the shotgun and bow are the only weapons allowed for deer.

In heavily-wooded areas such as scrub oak thickets, thick cedars, and pines, a single bullet will never reach its target, whereas the pellets from a load of buckshot probably will. In heavily populated areas shotguns are also the safest weapons because of their limited range.

Basically, shotguns are available as single-shot, double-barreled (and over and under), pump, semi-automatic, and bolt-action models.

The single shot, as I stated earlier (in the rifle section), has a definite advantage for the novice.

The double (double-barreled and over-and-under) shotguns are quite popular, particularly in England. They are also the most convenient gun you can buy. They're a breeze to clean, and to cross a fence or creek you simply break your gun open with the flick of a finger or thumb. The safety is on top, visible and easy to use when you bring your gun up to firing position.

One of the nicest features of doubles, besides their great balance, is that you can have one bore set at one choke and the other at another. For deer hunting with buckshot, you have a fast second shot with a tighter pattern if you need it.

Pumps are one of the best shotgun buys you can get. They are tough and easily repaired and very affordable; they offer interchangable barrels in a variety of styles, chokes, and lengths. They can also be mounted for a scope for use with slugs, if the hunter wishes. If a hunter does use slugs in his shotgun, a scope is recommended.

The semi-automatic is a dream to shoot because of its minimal recoil. Semi-automatics are favored by trap and skeet shooters because of this quality. However, as I mentioned in the rifle section, in the wrong hands they are useless.

The semi-automatic has an automatic ejection mechanism that seldom fails. They cost somewhat more than the pump models, and, like the pumps, they have interchangeable barrels of various styles, lengths, chokes, and gauges. They also can hold a scope for slug use.

Bolt actions, like single shots, make a great beginner's gun or utility gun because they are very inexpensive and generally safe to use. As on single-shot rifles, the action is strong—but that is where the similarity ends. Bolt-action shotguns are extremely slow to load— much slower than rifles—and are getting hard to locate in today's repeating-arms market.

GAUGES

Shotguns come in a variety of gauges, from the .410, which gives a very thin pattern but is a great training size, through the 28 gauge, 20 gauge, 16 gauge, 12 gauge, and the 10 gauge, which is almost obsolete except for use by duck hunters.

For whitetail hunting the 12 and 10 gauges are the only two

acceptable gauges, and in most areas they are the only ones allowed. The 16 gauge just does not have the power needed to do a dependable job.

Since we have a responsibility to make clean kills, it makes sense to use the most powerful of these short-range guns. There was once an 8 gauge but that died out years ago in favor of the 10. Now the 10 gauge is dying out because of the popularity of the 12.

One reason for the popularity of the 12 gauge is its versatility. It has power, handles a wide range of shot, has moderate recoil, and is as light as the 16 gauge. You can pack a 3-inch magnum shell into one, making it as good as a 10 gauge. They can be fitted for a 3½ inch shell. In short, they can do everything the other gauges do and do it without sacrificing anything.

BUCKSHOT AND SLUGS

Buckshot comes in a variety of sizes, from No. 4 to No. 000 magnum. Which size you should use depends upon how tight your shotgun holds a pattern with different size shot and loads. There is only one way to tell which shot and load to use: try all of them. To do this you must use at least three shells of each load and shoot them at heavy paper targets placed at least 30 yards away. The loads that yield the highest concentration of shot in the center of the target are the ones to use. If you have a double or an over and under, you should do this with each barrel.

In my double for instance, No. 4 buckshot holds best in the modified barrel, but No. 000 holds best in the full-choke barrel.

In testing the various loads you will find that shells with plastic collars consistently hold the best patterns.

Slugs shot from barrels designed for them are surprisingly accurate, even at 100 yards. When shot from barrels not made for them I have found them to be only marginal at 75 yards. If you use slugs, it would be of great advantage to mount a 2X scope on your shotgun.

When a slug hits it makes quite a hole. Unfortunately, because they are slow moving and hollow they usually don't do very well in heavy brush. It would benefit you to try out different makes of slugs. I have found the Brenneke brand to be the best. The casings do not split as did the S & W brand—and the lead held up better through brush.

HANDGUNS FOR WHITETAILS

Handgun hunters are increasing in numbers every year. Using handguns is a challenging sport. Like shotguns, handguns are well suited to the whitetail's habitat.

The handgun's short barrel requires a steady hand and plenty of self-control by the hunter to achieve reasonable accuracy even at 50 yards.

Since they are small and light, they are very maneuverable in brush country, and thus seem ideal—provided they have adequate power to penetrate brush. For this reason the handgun hunter should be armed with as heavy a weapon as he can safety handle.

Although a heavily-framed .38 Special will push a factory-make 110-grain semi-jacketed hollowpoint bullet at 1020 feet per second, the bullet won't hit hard enough to do a dependable job because it only produces 23 foot-pounds of energy at 50 yards. The smallest weapon that should be used is a .357 Magnum, pushing a 125-grain semi-jacketed hollowpoint bullet with 427 foot-pounds of energy at 50 yards. A 158-grain softpoint would be even better.

The .41 Remington Magnum with a 210-grain softpoint bullet is another top choice, as is the .44 Remington Magnum with a 180-grain semi-jacketed hollowpoint, or the 240-grain softpoint or semi-jacketed hollowpoint.

Hand-loaders that can increase the output of their cartridges to near rifle power benefit by making cleaner kills with softpoint bullets.

Handgun hunters should never use metal-jacketed, wadcutter, or hard-lead general-purpose bullets for deer hunting. The metal-jacketed and general-purpose bullets don't expand, and the wadcutter gives poor penetration and will not open up.

Neither yields enough shock.

I would like to mention here that you should buy only ammunition you are accustomed to or have loaded yourself. One time my cousin and a friend and I were plinking with his revolver using some .30-caliber imported ammunition. The cartridges shot flame-like powder two feet beyond the muzzle and out the breech! It didn't hurt the gun, but we all got powder burns.

MUSKETS

Black-powder hunting is another growing sport. More and more states have special deer seasons for muskets, and by taking advantage of them the sportsman can gain more recreation time and possibly additional meat in the freezer.

There are two types of black-powder rifles: the percussion, or "cap," and the popular flintlock.

The "cap lock" simplifies loading and offers high reliability in the field. However, this type of musket is not allowed in some states— apparently they feel it is too easy.

The flintlock, on the other hand, is welcome everywhere this type of hunting is allowed. It offers a bit more of a challenge because, for one thing, the powder is exposed and might not ignite in foul weather.

There are minimum caliber requirements: the .50-caliber musket is accepted nearly everywhere.

A musket's accuracy rivals that of a shotgun with slugs at 100 yards. There are rumors of 180-yard kills with muskets, but I haven't witnessed any of that distance. Kills of 125 yards are quite common in farm areas where unrestricted shots are possible.

SIGHTS AND SCOPES

The iron (open) sights that come on almost all rifles are usually of the shallow U or V shape. They are acceptable and for a long time were about the only kind of sight to be had. One drawback is that you have to line up three objects all at once: the rear sight, the front sight, and the target. Another is that your field of vision is restricted. As a deer moves along a trail, you often cannot see obstacles early enough to preplan an open shot while sighting. The front bead or mark should be no less than 3/32 inch across.

The peep sight is better for woods shooting than the open sight because it can be sighted faster. Your eye only has to focus on two objects: the front bead and the target. Your eye will automatically place the bead in the center of the aperature. If the sight has a large enough aperature, you will also have a full field of vision to work with.

The best sight of all is the telescopic scope. For a long time whitetail hunters avoided them because they thought that they would not be any good in heavily wooded areas. Once word got around about how fast they are to sight, however, and about how they enable the hunter to shoot in poor light, and about how they enable the hunter to see through brush to make better shots, hunters did not delay trying them out.

One of the first things that was found was that the lower powers—from 2X to 3X—are the best. That range of power offers more light and field of vision to the hunter. The higher-powered scopes are for varmint hunting.

Scopes are available in a variety of reticle designs such as the plain crosswire, dot, post, duplex, and rangefinder, to name a few.

Having the target and reticle on the same plane makes sighting nearly instantaneous. However, the reticle should be large enough to be found in a background of mixed cover or you will negate the scope's major advantage, speed. The large dot-and-post, or a combination having one large feature, is usually best.

Most hunters, including myself, like to have scope mounts that allow quick removal should we find it necessary to use open sights. There are sight-through mounts that let you use the iron sights by looking under the scope; there are quick-detachable mounts that release the scope; and there are swivel mounts that let you swing the scope out of the way. I prefer the latter—and have never had any trouble returning it to perfect zero.

SIGHTING A SCOPE THE FAST WAY

As common as scopes are, too many hunters don't know how properly to sight one in. This is one reason people miss so much game.

Very often, hunters take their rifle to a gunsmith to have it bore-sighted. This mechanical process is by no means accurate—all it does is put you somewhere on the paper at 100 yards.

Zeroing in your scope takes only a couple of minutes and can be done with just two bullets and the help of a friend.

The first step is to check all the scope mounting screws to make sure they are tight. Next, use a solid shooting bench and rest your rifle on some firm sandbags. At least two sandbags should be placed under the forearm of the rifle and another under the butt of the stock. Settle the rifle firmly onto the bags and then sight the reticle on the center of the target and dry-fire your rifle a few times to get the feel of it.

After a few such tries, you are ready. Don ear protection and glasses, if you have them, and load up. Get comfortable. Set the reticle on the middle of the target and squeeze off a round. Locate the hole your bullet made but keep the reticle on the bull's-eye.

Although you can do the nex step yourself, it works better if you have help. Keeping the reticle on the target center, have your friend turn either the windage or the elevation adjustment on the scope until it bisects the hole made by the first shot. Then do the same with the other adjustment. If you remained still while the adjustments were made, your scope should be zeroed-in. To make sure, fire a few more rounds.

PRACTICE

Once your scope is sighted in at a predetermined distance, you should practice shooting from the offhand position as much as possible. This position is the one that most hunters end up using whether they want to or not—including those hunters sitting in tree stands. This position is also the hardest one to master because there is little support for the rifle. Proper form is of the utmost importance. When hunting in rugged terrain, foot placement takes second place to arm placement, but the hunter should always try to keep his feet comfortably placed. Keep your right elbow (if right handed) up (parallel to your shoulder) and your left elbow under the forearm of the rifle. If you have a sling, use it and keep it tight. By tight I mean that the sling should have tension from the forearm of the rifle arm to your supporting arm (at the bicep muscle).

When hunting in unfamiliar territory you may find yourself with a longer shot than you have anticipated. If you have sighted in your rifle at much shorter distance, this can be a problem—especially if you have a low-velocity rifle such as a .30/30. Here a hunter should have a scope with a rangefinder or else a separate rangefinding device. I have found no one who can accurately estimate distances under varying conditions. A deer viewed across a canyon with no intervening objects or on a flat level plain with little or no vegetation will look closer than he really is. A deer in poor light will look farther away as will a deer viewed from above or below the hunter.

Focus-type rangefinding devices are better than the ones on scopes which use the split-wire method. The focus-types do not utilize the "average brisket" method and are therefore more accurate. Using a split-wire rangefinder, one places the animal's brisket between the two wires seen in the reticle and adjusts the scope so that one wire is along the back and the other at the base of the brisket. You then read what is supposed to be the accurate distance.

The problem here is that different animals have different sized briskets. For example, the brisket could measure from 14 to 21 inches, depending on the size of the deer. The average is 18 inches, and it is this average that scope manufacturers use to calculate the distance for the two-wire system. For deer hunting, it is an acceptable method which will give accuracy below 300 yards. However, this kind of scope is expensive, and you may want to give a bit of thought to its limitations if you intend to use it on such larger animals as elk or moose, as these animals have a greater range of brisket size. Accurate yardage calculations using an average are thus harder to achieve.

The scope or sight should always be sighted in at the longest range you expect to encounter. I say this because, should you have to make a quick second shot at a running animal, you will have a tendency to sight on the animal instead of over it, and will therefore shoot low. By sighting at the longest expected range, you should be on the money.

Some models have an automatic bullet compensator that lets you hold the reticle on target rather than guess how high over the target to aim.

One more thing about long-range shooting: If at all possible, don't. Long-range shooting invites problems. But if you do, make sure your rifle is steady, the path to the target unobstructed, and the bullet's trajectory known. Some experienced hunters I know tape this technical information onto the butt of their gun for quick reference.

PRACTICE HITTING A MOVING TARGET

During the firearms season, few deer are shot standing still—often as not they are moving at quite a pace. Considering that deer can run as fast as 40 mph, you can see that hitting this brush-loving critter as he weaves through the trees and thickets can be quite tricky. As big as they are, at times they are as tough to hit as rabbits in high grass.

There are some ways to practice to come out on top. One is to practice at a trap house or to break some hand-thrown clay birds before the season. This should be done even if you use a rifle, musket, or handgun, because it gets you familiar with swing and timing. Small-

Hold your sights on an opening (X) that the deer is headed for. When the deer enters the opening, he's yours.

game hunting is another great way to get your reflexes in shape and sharpen your eye.

If you wish to practice with your rifle or pistol, try this method: Take an old tire and put a round piece of cardboard in the center where the wheel was and make a 4-inch bull's-eye in the center. Now, find a slope with a good backstop. Using the load you plan to shoot, pace off about 50 yards. Have a well-hidden-and-protected companion roll the tire down the hill for you to shoot at. It helps to have a bumpy course for the tire to traverse as it rolls down the hill, since deer jump as they run.

In heavy cover, there is only one dependable way to nail your deer: hold your sights on an opening that the deer is headed for and when it enters that opening, shoot. This method works because you have a full view of the area and will not hit unseen obstructions as you swing the weapon.

5

Archery

Hunting with bow and arrow is to me the ultimate challenge. The bow hunter puts himself on an even level with his quarry. He works harder to get closer to his target and is often frustrated in his efforts. His reward is a better understanding of nature and the satisfaction of doing things the hard way. When he succeeds, he knows he has earned it.

Like all other sports, archery undergoes evolution. New and improved products are introduced regularly and once in a while an improvement will have a tremendous impact.

One such improvement is the compound bow.

This box, with its cables, pulleys, and eccentric wheels, enables the archer to hold his arrow at full draw longer than with a standard bow because full draw requires 20–50 percent less effort. The lessened draw allows the archer to use a higher weight bow and heavier arrows for better penetration.

Another advantage of the compound bow is its ability to send an arrow to its target about 50 percent faster than a conventional recurved bow. This potential is misunderstood or misused by many hunters, however. The novice, impressed by the potential speed of his arrow, often uses lighter arrows to achieve a flatter trajectory and actually loses vital penetration.

When I first laid eyes on this cumbersome-looking contraption, I had my doubts about it. It was heavy and there were so many adjustments to make accurately that I had to wonder what would happen if it were dropped. After shooting it a few times, however, I was well aware of its advantages and was willing to forego my misgivings. My lovely wife Susan saw the twinkle in my eye and, lo and behold, somehow it was my birthday.

After shooting a recurve most of my life, I had to learn to shoot all over again. The compound handled quite differently and, I must admit, I was tempted at times to switch back to the recurve. But that was then; now I would never consider it.

The compound bow comes in many styles and materials and is by far the leading seller and probably will continue to be for quite some time.

But there are some hunters who prefer to keep things simple. Since deer are usually killed with a bow at short ranges (10 to 25 yards), these hunters would rather use the traditional longbow (straight limb) or recurve. The loss of a few feet per second at short distances, is a minimal disadvantage. The traditionalists prefer to retain the crisp, smooth reliability of the conventional bow. Such great pioneers of bow hunting as Dr. Saxton Pope, Art Young, and Howard Hill all used the long bow; world-famous archer Fred Bear still uses a recurve. You have to admit, all of these men have accomplished amazing feats with conventional equipment, so it is not to be taken lightly.

In fact, straight and recurve bows do have certain advantages over compounds. They are not as temperental: a poor release with a conventional bow will not be as noticeable as one with a compound because the arrow leaves the string very soon after release. With a compound bow, the arrow remains on the string longer, and so a good release is imperative for accuracy. Conventional bows are simple to care for and are extremely light; they are less likely to be damaged in a fall. They are smoother shooting than any compound I have tried. The recurves of today are much better made and more versatile than earlier models. They come in takedown form and offer a variety of limbs to fit your needs.

The most important consideration in selecting a bow is draw weight. Use the maximum weight you can handle. A good way to determine this is to come to full draw and hold. If you can hold longer than five seconds, the weight should be OK for you. Also, a hunter should move up in weight as he gains strength and ability.

ARROWS AND PENETRATION

An archer harvests his deer by causing massive hemorrhaging. The more vital tissues severed, the more efficient and humane the kill. Razor-sharp arrowheads and deep penetration are the keys to this goal. Since draw weight is often determined by the strength of the archer's muscles, he must try to make the best use of whatever driving force he has. So let's start with arrow selection.

There are a variety of arrow types available to the bow hunter. Among these are different grades of aluminum, different types and combinations of fiberglass, wood (cedar), and graphite. They each have appealing characteristics.

Aluminum is light and uniformly made. If bent, an aluminum arrow usually can be repaired. Fiberglass is heavier than aluminum but more durable. Wood is even heavier and is not durable—however, it is the most economical to replace. Graphite is durable, very light, but not very available in sporting goods stores.

Penetration being one of the keys to successful bow hunting, which arrow will deliver the deepest penetration? The answer can be complex, especially if the hunter decides to experiment and fine-tune his equipment. (All archers should take the time to do this but unfortunately most don't. They buy whatever the sporting goods dealer suggests.)

I made some tests for penetration using standard hunting arrows purchased from a nearby sporting-goods shop. The arrows were matched in spine for my compound bow set at 55 lbs. Each was fitted with identical field tips. For a target, I combined four sections, each 2¼ inches thick, of a tough polyethylene called Ethafoam. I chose this material because of its uniformity. The results were as follows: The deepest penetration came from my fiberglass (Graphlex) arrows with feathers. These penetrated from 2⅜ inches to an even 3 inches. Fiberglass arrows with plastic vanes came in second with penetration ranging from 1¾ to 2⁹⁄₁₆ inches.

The heavier gauge aluminum arrows came next, with penetration ranging from 1¼ to 1⅞ inches with feathers, and from 1¼ to 1½ inches with vanes.

Wood came next with penetration ranging from ⅝ to 1 inch with feathers and from ⅝ to ⅞ of an inch with vanes. The poor performance of the wood arrows seemed to be due to their slowness. The lack of speed resulting from a 55-lb. bow prohibited full use of the arrows' energy potential.

Lightweight aluminum arrows came in next but very close to the wooden arrows. I got penetration ranging from ½ to ⅞ of an inch with feathers and ³⁄₁₆ to ½ of an inch with vanes. I tried a few arrows with four-vane fletching and got the poorest result, probably due to their added drag. This slower arrow registered penetration of only ¼ to ⅜ of an inch. As you can see, it nearly failed to penetrate at all!

The graphite arrows with feathers could only equal the economy grade aluminum arrows with the four fletched plastic vanes. The graphite arrows with vanes barely left measurable marks on this tough target.

Another key factor which determines penetration is the type of arrowhead. Poor choice in arrowhead selection can make even a good arrow as bad as the poorest arrow. So let's take a closer look at this factor.

Basically there are two types of arrowheads for deer hunting on the market today. These are the conventional, non-sharpened heads (you must hone these to a razor edge), and the pre-sharpened kind, which usually have replaceable razor blades.

The conventional types are strong and, if you keep them honed to razor sharpness, will prove to be very dependable. The only trouble is that few hunters can or will take the time to get them that sharp. Penetration can be increased on conventional arrowheads by serrating them—filing notches along the edges like those on a steak knife. Serrated edges cut faster, yielding deeper penetration.

The replaceable razor-blade types are a great aid to the hunter. If you have ever cut yourself with a razor blade you know just how hard it is to stop the bleeding. Since the object is hemorrhaging, you can see one of the advantages of this kind of head. Another is that you can replace the razor blades should they be damaged or dulled.

The ideal arrowhead should have at least three cutting edges, since a multiple-blade cut does not clot as easily as a two-blade cut. It should also have a point that won't bend, break, or flatten out when it hits bone. The arrowhead should have a cutting width of at least one inch from blade edge to blade edge, and each cutting edge should be at least an inch long. The blade length is not as important as its width. The cutting edges should be as close to the point as possible.

There is at least one replaceable-blade arrowhead that is so thick at the point that it reduces penetration considerably. I am not out to discredit the people that produce the head, so I will not mention its name.

I should also point out that the more blades an arrowhead has, the poorer the arrow's flight, because of added weight and drag. The arrow will wind plane (the blades catch too much air and steer off course) and have a tendency to dive early. Three-blade arrowheads fly better and seem to produce deeper penetration, according to a test I conducted.

In the arrowhead penetration test, all the heads were tested on the same arrow and shot into the same material I used in the arrow test described earlier.

The deepest penetrating arrowhead was one called the Micro-Point. It is of the pre-sharpened, razor-blade type and made of virtually-indestructable, glass-filled polycarbonate with a small case-hardened steel point. The three blades were carbon steel. This arrowhead had excellent flight characteristics and accuracy. I believe that its penetration was deepest because its razor blades were more than 25 percent closer to the point that its nearest competitor.

The results were so close in the rest of the replaceable-blade arrowheads that it would not be fair to mention brands. At any rate, all the remaining three-blade arrowheads out-performed the other kinds.

The three-blade non-razor (conventional) heads gave good penetration *if* razor sharp. As the number of blades increased, the penetration decreased in all instances. A couple two-blade heads were tested but none equaled the three-blade razor heads.

As one can see, using the proper combination of arrow and arrowhead can greatly affect penetration. The lower the bow weight used, the more critical is the choice of arrow and arrowhead.

It would behoove the archer to conduct his own experiments.

CORRECT ARROW LENGTH

After you have decided on the type of arrow you will hunt with, you have to determine your draw length. Draw length is the distance from where the bowstring rests in the nock of the arrow when held at full draw to the face of the bow (beyond the arrow shelf). To measure this distance, most archery shops and sporting goods dealers use an old lightweight bow and an arrow marked off in inches. Simply draw the marked arrow back to your anchor point and read the draw length on the face of the bow.

Most hunters, including myself, add one inch to the draw length to arrive at arrow length. This prevents the sharp blades of the arrowhead from injuring the fingers in the event of an overdraw which, unfortunately, does happen from time to time when one gets a bit excited. If a marked arrow is not available, have a friend mark an arrow for you while you hold at full draw.

Should a bow and arrow not be available, there are other ways to measure draw length. The easiest is to hold your hands palm to palm with your arms stretched forward. An arrow of proper length will reach from the center of your chest to your finger tips.

Another method is to stand facing at 90 degrees to a wall and extend your clenched fist against the wall. Turn your head so it now looks down your arm to the wall. Have some one measure the distance from your anchor-point to the wall. (This method does not allow for your arm caving in under stress, so it will be long by at least one inch.)

Still another method to determine the arrow length is to use the spread-arm method. With the aid of a long tape measure or a board marked off in inches, simply extend your arms outward to the sides and measure from finger tip to finger tip then compare this measurement to the chart.

Spread measurement	Arrow length
57"–59"	24"–25"
60"–62"	25"–26"
63"–65"	26"–27"
66"–68"	27"–28"
69"–71"	28"–29"
72"–74"	29"–30"
75"–77"	30"–31"

ARROW SPINE

One of the most important factors in accurate and consistent shooting is arrow spine. Simply, arrow spine is the stiffness of the arrow, which is determined by the length of the arrow and the draw weight.

To understand arrow spine, you must realize what takes place when an arrow is released. The force of the bow pushes the arrow forward, causing it to bend. The arrow must recover its shape to fly straight, and this recovering quality is known as spine. If an arrow shoots to the left of the target, it is recovering too soon. The arrow has "too much spine." If the arrow shoots to the right, then it is recovering too slowly and has too little spine. If your arrows land consistently to one side or the other, you probably have improperly spined arrows.

You can check the spine of your arrow by using a simple formula.

For draw lengths of 28 inches: match the arrow's spine to the bow's weight.

For draw lengths shorter than 28 inches, use this simple calculation:

1. Divide your bow's draw weight at 28 inches by 20.
2. Multiply this number by the number of inches (or fractions thereof) your draw is shorter than 28 inches.
3. Subtract this number from the bow's draw weight at 28 inches. (This gives you your draw weight at your draw length.)
4. Match your arrow spine to the final draw weight number.

Example: Bow weight = 50 lbs. Draw length = 27½ inches
   50 ÷ 20 = 2.5 lb.
   2.5 × .5" = 1.25 lb.
   50 − 1.25 = #48.75 at 27½ draw length

For draw lengths longer than 28 inches you use the following calculation:

1. Divide the bow's draw weight at 28 inches by 20
2. Multiply this number by the number of inches (and fractions thereof) that your draw is longer than 28 inches.
3. Add this number to the bow's draw weight at 28 inches.
4. Match arrow spine to final draw weight number.

Example: Bow weight = 50 lb.—Draw length = 29½
50 lb. – 20 = 2.5 lb.
2.5 × 1.5 = 3.75
50 lb. + 3.75 = #53.75 at 29½ draw length

Experimentation by the individual archer will eventually lead to variations on standard calculations.

BOW HUNTING WITH SIGHTS

For many hunters the bow sight is one of the greatest shooting aids ever to appear. As with gunsights, once a bow sight is sighted in at a given distance, the arrow should hit its target every time at that distance. I've seen sights improve the target scores of many people. Unlike gunsights, bow sights will normally have multiple adjustment pins (usually four) for windage and elevation. This is useful because an arrow is much slower than a bullet, and thus has a much shorter range and much more variable trajectory.

Because most good bowmen seldom shoot more than 30 yards, the sight pins are normally set in 10 yard increments. Ten-yard, 20-yard, 30-yard, and 40-yard adjustments are possible. Once you have the pins set for your shooting style and equipment, you must be sure to judge shooting distances correctly and sight with the correct pin for that distance.

This creates a problem for some archers who are poor judges of distance and won't take the time to learn how to do it. The best way to learn is to practice: walk a few yards counting your steps as you go, then measure to see just how far you have traveled. Do this as often as possible at varying distances, and, after a few hours, you will become quite good at estimating distances of under 100 yards.

For the hunter that can't judge distances accurately, even with practice, there are several sights on the market that incorporate range-finders. They work on the two-wire principle, but differ from rifle scopes in that they have four sets of rangefinder wires or markings instead of one. Each set marks 10-yard increments, starting at 10 yards and working up to 40. They are usually color-coded to help you identify the correct pin, once you have determined the yardage. As with the scope, you find the set of rangefinder wires that comes closest to fitting the size of the brisket, then select the correct pin. You should then be on target.

Whichever kind of sight you choose, it should be of sturdy construction, because it will be subject to quite a bit of punishment over a period of time. The sight should be screwed to the bow, never taped. The sight pins should have a positive locking device such as a screw or nut. Friction and adhesive devices are a gamble because they tend to move—after going through all the time and trouble to sight them in properly, I am sure you don't want them to move just as you are about to release on your long-awaited deer!

There is one major flaw in using sights for hunting. Deer are seldom immobile, so the distance between you and your target is constantly changing. When I received my compound bow several years ago, I put a sight on it in hope of improving my accuracy. As I said earlier, I had to learn to shoot all over again. After a few weeks with the sight, I could put six arrows in a match-book at 20 yards. That was pretty fair shooting but it played havoc with my arrows! However, when the season arrived, I found that sights were not for me. My mind is so intent upon moving slowly, watching deer approach, searching for other deer which may be nearby (which may give me away), and thinking about when to draw (and when I draw, I concentrate on my target and am concerned only about when to release), that I forget all about the pins. I kept them for two seasons and each time the result was the same. So, I removed them.

But for an archer who doesn't use instinct, sights are the best way to score.

THE BOW QUIVER

There are many kinds of quivers available. There is the long, deep, pouch type that is carried across your back—like Indians use . . . but unfortunately this type of quiver has three bad features: It is a bit noisy because the arrows bang against each other; the exposed arrow ends catch on branches; and it requires exaggerated arm movement to extract a second arrow. Each could spook deer.

The pocket quiver is another type. Although quiet, it also allows the arrows to catch on brush, and so won't do for hunting, either.

The best quiver is the bow-attached quiver. It carries three to eight arrows and, if secured properly, is quiet. The bow quiver also holds the arrows in front of you so you can see them and prevent them from getting caught in brush. It has a cup-shaped end that protects the

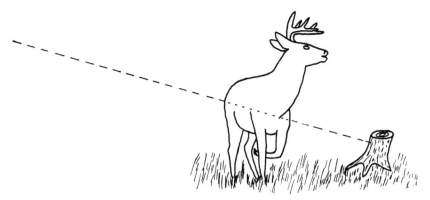

Shoot *through* the deer. By concentrating on an object, or the ground, just on the other side of the deer, an archer may find that the worry of misjudging distance and arrow trajectory will be greatly reduced. It is always safer to shoot low than to try to determine exact distance.

arrowheads (and you), and dampens the vibration when you release your arrow. The location of the quiver also allows you to extract arrows quickly, quietly, and with little motion. Since a hunter must carry extra arrows into the woods, the bow-attached quiver is the ideal way to do it.

A tip: Whether you shoot with finger tabs or a shooting glove, be sure that you have not worn deep creases in the finger joints. Deep creases often cause poor releases.

THE MECHANICAL RELEASE

As I mentioned earlier, on a compound bow the arrow release is very critical because the arrow starts out slowly, then gains momentum. This extra time makes a smooth release important. A mechanical release is just what the name implies: a hand-held object which holds and then releases the bowstring. Mechanical releases act like triggers: some loose the arrow with the press of a button or lever, while others employ a string-and-metal spike mechanism.

The spike type of release uses a string (looped around the bowstring) which slides off a metal appendage. When the string is freed it releases the bowstring and sends the arrow on its way. Since you can't see this happening, the exact time at which the arrow will be released is not precisely known and you must make an educated guess.

When shooting at a moving target hunters often try to rush this type of release, and the results are similar to those when a rifleman jerks the trigger on his weapon.

For hunting purposes, if you decide that a release is for you (and it is allowed by law), a lever or button release is the best choice. With so many variables in the woods—the stop-and-go movement of the deer and the ever-changing wind and brush configurations, you need to know exactly when your arrow will be released.

Some hunters don't believe release aids should be used because they make hunting too "mechanical." Although I don't use a release, I find myself disagreeing with them. Anything that can increase accuracy should be encouraged for the benefit of the sport.

SHOOTING BASICS

If you are new to archery it is important that you first learn proper form. By learning the basics you can gain the confidence to develop other shooting forms needed for quick clean kills in the field. The form I will show you is basic and easily learned (accuracy will come with practice and patience).

1. If you are right-handed, hold the bow in your left hand. Your right hand will be pulling back the string and arrow. The bow fits in the V between the left index finger and thumb, which should form a loose ring around the bow handle. Other fingers should be relaxed.
2. Stand with your left side toward the target and place your feet comfortably apart facing away from the target at a right angle.
3. Nock your arrow (it should fit snugly on the string) with the odd feather (usually a different color) pointing away from the bow (so it won't strike the arrow rest as it passes). If you are using a four-fletched arrow, it doesn't have an odd feather, so it doesn't matter which way it is nocked. The nocked arrow should be below and against the nocking point on your bow string. (If your string doesn't have a nocking point on it then you should have one installed.)
4. Pull the string lightly with the first three fingers of your right hand with the arrow lying lightly between the index finger and middle

finger. The thumb and little fingers are not used. Your wrist should be relaxed.

5. Keep your head raised and look at the center of the target.
6. Raise your bow arm and draw up to shoulder level.
7. The bottom of your bow arm elbow should be turned away from the string and the elbow held stiff.
8. *Using your back and shoulder muscles,* draw the arrow back until your index finger touches the corner of your mouth. Your thumb will slide under and behind your jaw. Concentrate on your target.
9. Keep tension on back muscles and drawing arm, and your wrist relaxed and straight, while aiming. The bow is now pulling against the base of your bow hand. Keep your grip loose, using your index and thumb, and your other fingers free.
10. This is the critical part. *Keep your anchor point firm.* Put *more* tension on your back and shoulder muscles, then relax your fingers, letting the string roll off your fingers while you keep your eyes on the center of your target.
11. Keep your eyes on the center of the target and keep your bow arm in the release position. Let the tension of your back and shoulder muscles draw your fingers back along your neck. Hold this position until you hear the arrow strike the target.

As early as possible, try to get some instruction from a professional. He can help prevent the development of incorrect shooting habits and increase your score dramatically. If professional help is not available, try joining an archery club. They will no doubt have some very fine archers who would enjoy helping you.

PRACTICE HINTS

The average bowman begins to practice two months or more before hunting season. He knows he has to be sharp because he is aware that with his short-range equipment it is the first shot that will count and that he may not get another.

The most serious hunters practice shooting in a variety of positions: kneeling, standing, body twisted, and—most important of all—from an elevated platform. Most hunters will be in tree stands when the season opens.

They don't shoot at targets with big circles on them either. Rather,

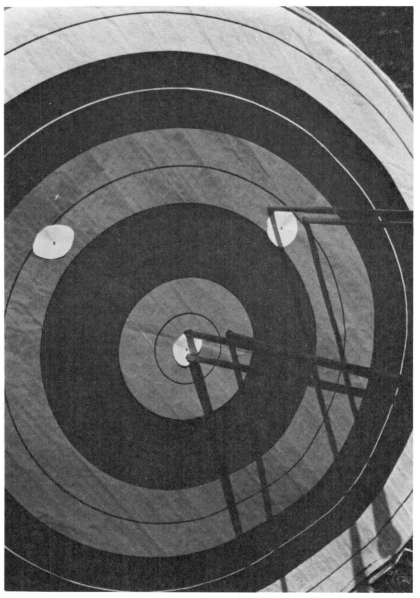

Train your eyes to shoot at small spots, not large objects.

they shoot at one- or two-inch targets. The experienced hunter knows that the smaller the target, the more crucial eye concentration becomes. He doesn't shoot at the whole deer, just a small spot on the deer. Also, the experienced hunter realizes that he may have to thread the arrow through narrow openings in the brush to hit that spot, so, shooting at small targets is his best form of practice.

As the season nears the serious hunter dresses up his bow with string and or cable silencers and keeps arrows in the now-attached bow quiver. He makes sure that the arrow rest is of the bristle or other soft types so the arrow won't make noise as it is drawn back. Silence and confidence that he's shooting with proper gear are imperative to the serious hunter.

6

Optics

Optical instruments offer hunters and wildlife observers an advantage in locating bigger bucks and more productive trails and in planning a stalking strategy. With optics one can see into brush better than without them. If you have ever seen deer browsing in brush or fields, but been unable to see their heads clearly enough to determine if they had any "bone" showing between their ears, then you know another reason for using optics: curiosity. When hunting from a stand, optics tell you in advance if something is coming your way, what it is, and which trail it will be taking.

Four sizes that are commonly used in deer hunting: 6 × 30, 7 × 35, 7 × 50, and 8 × 30.

The magnification power, or the number of times the glass increases the size of what you can see with your human eye, is represented by the first number. For example, an 8 × 30 binocular will make the image you are looking at appear 8 times closer than it really is.

The second figure is the diameter of the objective lens in millimeters. The size of the objective lens determines how much light the lens admits, and therefore determines how well you can see the image.

If you have a chance to view several binoculars, you will find that a 30mm is more than adequate in heavy woods, but a 50mm is much better because it admits more light. The 30mm has one advantage over the 50: it is smaller and more compact. In bow hunting that is a big plus.

Of the popular sizes, 6 × 30 is best for the bowman because he usually hunts when the foliage is still heavy. The less the magnification, the better the viewing through brush.

The 8 × 30 is the largest a hunter would want to use in a wooded area, because the higher magnification amplifies all the little movements of your body—such as arm movement and breathing—and therefore defeats its purpose. With optics above 8 power, you may need a solid rest to hold the glass still enough for a clear sighting.

The all-around favorites are the 7 × 35 and the 7 × 50—medium-power glasses that handle very well in mixed terrain.

The field of view—often designated with the other numbers—is the width of the area you see through the glass at a designated distance (usually 1,000 feet).

There are two opinions on how to use the field of view. Some hunters like a narrow field of view, preferring to scan an area by moving the glass back and forth. Others, like myself, prefer a wider field of vision so we can see more at one time.

I look at it this way: anytime you have to move the glasses, you are apt to miss or pass by something too quickly. Once you scan past an object, all too often you cannot find it again right away. I'd rather have a wider field of view and let my eyes scan the magnified field. This way I can find the small details—such as a flicker of an ear—at the edge of the magnified field—and not lose the sight once spotted. Scanning, I may miss completely.

A monocular is a great tool for the bowhunter because it is compact. The view is somewhat harder to control because you are only using one eye, but considering the lower cost and convenience, monoculars can be a real asset. Ranging, Inc., offers a 6 × 18 optic which can be conveniently worn on your wrist.

When buying binoculars, always make sure that the glasses are coated. This cuts down reflections and brings in the true colors, as well as giving a more brilliant image. The coating should have a purple-violet tint. If the coating is too thin it will have a yellow or amber tint; if the lenses are blue, the coating may be too thick. A good way to check for a complete coating job by the manufacturer is to hold the binoculars so that they catch the reflection of an overhead flourescent light. If the reflection that comes through the lens is pure white instead of the color which is supposed to be on the lens, then at least one lens surface has not been coated.

The focusing mechanism should fit your needs. Some binoculars have a single knob which moves both lenses, while others have oculars that adjust individually.

Alignment must also be perfect. After correctly adjusting the binoculars, view a horizontal straight line such as a telephone wire or window frame. Then move the binoculars away from your eyes so that you can see two separate images. Follow this by spreading the barrels away from each other to see if the straight line remains continuous in both views. If the images appear out of alignment you may end up with eyestrain or other visual discomfort.

Image quality should be crisp. By viewing small thin lines close together you can get a reasonable idea of image quality. If the lines seem to blend together try a different binocular.

Moveable parts should work smoothly and the binoculars should have rubber seals where moving parts connect (i.e., at the focusing mechanism). All non-moving parts should have rubber gaskets or ''O'' rings. Wax or grease seals will break down after a short period of time and will allow moisture—which causes fogging—and dust to enter.

Try to ensure that the pair of binoculars you buy fits you. Try several until you get a pair that feels right.

Finally, buy the best your budget will allow. In optics, you usually get what you pay for.

7

Camouflage

Camouflage is essential to the bowhunter. Unlike the gun hunter, the bowman must get very close to his deer (usually under 30 yards). To do this successfully, the bowman must remain completely hidden from deer and other forest creatures. If the hunter doesn't look like part of his immediate surroundings, every move he makes will be detected long before the deer comes into range.

For the hunter to blend in with his surroundings, he must wear the right clothes. They should be of varying greens and browns, and have patterns that resemble the surrounding vegetation. For instance, when you are hunting in pines your camouflage outfit should be dark green and brown and have a horizontal pattern. A rounded-leaf pattern with a tan background will stick out immediately. However, hunters are often mobile and hunt varying terrain. It isn't practical, or necessary for that matter, to carry a change of outfits just to blend in with the terrain. What is needed is an understanding of how different colors and patterns are seen in the black-and-white world of the whitetail. With this knowledge you can adjust your camouflage to any situation.

As I mentioned in an earlier chapter whitetails have very few

Notice how the darker colored pullover mask is better suited to use in evergreens than the basic leaf pattern with the light brown or beige base.

cones in their retinas. Since cones distinguish color, we must assume that the whitetail is effectively color-blind. This, however, does not mean that you can wear any color in the woods, because different colors register as different shadings in the black-and-white world.

White is a warning color to the whitetail, and easiest seen. This means that blond hair and fair skin should be covered or masked with darker colors. Blue, red, and dark green tend to show dark. Light colors such as yellow, orange, or light green show as gray. Flourescent colors such as hunters' orange, show an unnatural brilliance. Unless you hunt in an area with a lot of white blossoms, stay away from flourescent colors, as there is virtually nothing natural that you can blend in with.

Leaves of plants and trees are lighter on the bottom than on the top and reflect quite a bit of light on a breezy day. But even then there are more dark areas than light. What this indicates is that when you are using camouflage, dark colors should always predominate, and always in irregular patterns.

A lot of hunters go into the woods wearing a standard camouflage outfit consisting of a hat, jacket, and pants. That's OK if they remain motionless in a tree stand. In fact some hunters, including myself, wear only half the outfit when hunting from a tree stand. However, if you hunt from the ground, there are four more areas that must be covered . . .

The face is probably the most important part of the body to cover when hunting from the ground. The cheek bones, chin, and nose (bridge and sides) are oily and reflect light. When using camouflage grease or paint, these areas should be well covered in broken patterns. Everyone blinks, especially when nervous, so put some grease on your eyelids too. The colors should be brown, black, and green—in short dabs and lines. For those of you who prefer not to use camouflage grease, there are face masks of varying designs which are just as effective.

The hands are another often-overlooked area. Either wear gloves to cover the hands' glare or use camouflage grease in short dabs or short horizontal lines.

The bow too should be camouflaged. On numerous occasions I have spotted other hunters by their bows' reflections. If glare is noticeable to me, just think how noticeable it is to the deer and what this unnatural sight must mean to them! There are several ways to camouflage bow limbs. One way is to purchase camouflage tape or a camouflage cloth cover; another is to spray the limbs with non-reflective paint. If you decide to paint your bow, be sure to break up the image by making several light (yellow or light green) streaks of leaf patterns on the limbs.

The aluminum arrow is another item that may need to be camouflaged before you go into the woods. After repeated practice sessions,

The importance of being in the shade is clearly illustrated by comparing these two pictures. In the brighter picture, notice the glare on the hunter's face, hands, and on the arrows, where the finish has been worn off from practice shooting. Also, although the bow has been painted with camouflage paint in leaf patterns, there is not enough yellow or light green in the pattern to break up the image. The result is a long, unbroken image.

As this picture illustrates, a hunter wearing camouflage doesn't need very much cover to blend in with his surroundings. However, the lack of a well camouflaged bow and the aluminum arrows with their worn finish will give him away with even the slightest movement. A novice bow hunter using no camouflage or improperly camouflaged equipment should hunt from a tree and not from the ground.

the coating on most aluminum arrows will wear off where the arrow has penetrated the target. If not retouched, the bare aluminum will reflect light, making quite a glare. Reflections are unnatural and should be covered; a light spray painting is all that is usually necessary.

To all the things I've mentioned that need camouflage, I would like to add one that doesn't: the arrow crest. It should be brightly colored—even white. Why? So you will be able to track your arrow to its target. By keeping track of your arrow's flight you can tell immediately if you scored a hit and where. Should you miss, a white crest is easier to find than the flourescent, especially when mixed up with colorful autumn leaves.

Don't worry about the white crest spooking deer. Neither I nor the other hunters I know who use a white crest have ever attributed a spooking to it. If you have doubts, cover your arrow crest with a section of camouflage cloth. There are commercial arrow covers available for just that purpose.

That you have camouflaged yourself doesn't mean you can walk through the middle of a field or along the crest of a hill or down the middle of a road without being spotted. You must constantly be aware of your surroundings and hide your silhouette just as if you were not camouflaged. Most important of all, stay in shadow—or at least behind leafy branches.

8

Boots

I don't know how many miles we walked that day, but I do know that they were hard miles through some of the thickest brush and swamps the pinelands had to offer.

When we arrived back at the cabin, the first thing most of the men did was kick off their boots and rub their sore feet. Curiously, nearly all the men with sore feet were wearing all-rubber boots with man-made "fleece" lining.

The men who kept their boots on and didn't complain were the ones with leather hunting boots which were well broken in before the season.

I was only twelve years old at the time and was one of the poor souls with rubber boots. They didn't "give" when I walked, they were heavy, and they had a habit of pulling my socks down to my toes— it seemed I was forever taking them off to adjust my socks. After two seasons of this I finally learned my lesson. Just before the following small game season, I purchased a pair of good lightweight boots from a reputable shoe store.

The dealer, who not only sold but had worn many kinds of boots, from street to mountaineering, had some sound advice to give about choice, fit, and breaking.

Boot choice should reflect the kind of terrain you intend to hunt. For instance, if you intend to hunt moose or deer in swamp land, you need a pair of well-fitted hip boots. By "well-fitted" I mean firm (but comfortable) around the foot and ankle so heavy muck won't pull them off your feet. Loose-fitting hip boots will drive you crazy by the end of the day.

If you are headed for high rocky terrain, lightweight hiking boots with thick lug soles offer great footing, and thus would be a wise choice.

For winter use, especially if you are going to be hunting from a tree stand, the intelligent choice would be boots with full felt linings. They will keep your feet warm and you can replace wet linings before the next day's hunt. They are quite bulky, but satisfactory for the immobile hunter.

If you do a lot of walking in not too steep or marshy terrain, choose a general-purpose boot. The general-purpose hunting boot may be insulated or not, and have lugged or non-lugged soles. For snow-covered terrain lugged soles are best. Boots should be made of leather and be as light as possible.

The most expensive boots are not always the best, so it would be wise to save your warranty card. One pair of boots I purchased had to be returned twice and I still am not satisfied with them. I have since purchased an old favorite of mine, which I have found much less expensive and far more dependable than the so-called "top of the line" boots. That "top of the line" insulated boot is now used only in emergencies.

A boot's fit is of utmost importance. Some people buy boots a size or half size larger than their shoe size to allow for heavy socks and swelling feet. This is *not* the way to go, especially if you buy leather boots. Boots should feel comfortable without tightness. Too large boots cause blisters—and make your socks bunch up under the arch of your foot.

Whether you purchase rubber, leather, or a combination of the two, a hunting boot should have a minimum of four inches of ankle support. It will not only protect your ankle from sprains, it will keep out foreign matter as you walk through the fields and woods.

Stockings are a very important item and should be considered when you try on boots. There are a number of kinds of hunting socks on the market today, all of which claim to keep your feet warm and probably will, if your feet stay dry. But once the socks are wet, even from perspiration, you'll have cold feet, insulated boots or not.

There is only one sock for the outdoorsman and that is wool. The higher the wool content the better (never less than 75 percent). Even wet wool will keep your feet warm. If wool makes you itch you can use a pair of thin cotton or nylon socks as liners—you may experience cold feet however.

BREAKING IN

There are two basic ways to break in leather boots. One is to wear them around the house, or to work, for about a month. (The socks you wear should be the same as you will wear when the season opens.)

A faster way to break in boots is to fill them with water (hot, but not boiling) for about ten minutes. Then empty them out and let them drain for at least five minutes. Then put them on over the same socks you will use during the season and walk them dry for at least eight hours.

A more enjoyable method is to put the boots on (with the correct socks) and walk through the wettest swamp area you can find while spotting deer or hunting small game. At the end of the day, you will not only have enjoyed yourself, you will have completely broken in your boots. The water break-in process works on insulated as well as noninsulated boots.

Proper care of leather boots is a continual process and well worth the time it takes, especially considering the high cost of boots. The key to boot care is preventing the leather from drying out and cracking. There are a number of boot dressings on the market such as silicone, mink oil, wax, and combinations of all of these. Whichever dressing you choose, the important thing is to use it often.

9

Odor Problems

The olfactory system of the whitetail is the only sense that is completely independent in its ability to trigger an alarm. Should a whitetail see movement, it will listen and smell to determine if there is danger. When a whitetail hears a noise, it will often try to see you and smell you. However, if a whitetail smells you, at any distance, it's all over. The deer wastes no time in vacating the area. It needs no other confirmation . . .

A typical hunt morning: The hunter takes a bath or shower, using a deodorant soap and a scented shampoo. He takes his clothes out of the closet or from the corner of the tent and gets dressed. He grabs something to eat and has a cigarette or two. Perhaps he builds a fire or at least puts a log on it. Now he is ready to stalk his deer.

After hours of hard work, sweat, and skillful tracking, he spots a fine buck just 200 yards away. As he slowly eases himself into position for a shot, the inevitable happens: the wind shifts and carries his scent toward the trophy animal. But the hunter's not worried. He took a bath, even though it was several hours ago. He is using a dependable buck lure. Everything is in his favor.

The buck lifts his head and looks directly at him. His tail goes up and so does the hair on his back. He has scented danger. Once the odor is picked up by his sensitive nose, he needs no confirmation by sight or sound. He lays his ears back and leaves in a flash.

The hunter returns to camp that night still trying to figure out what went wrong.

Some of the answers are obvious and some aren't. The hunter's first mistake was not taking the deer's highly developed olfactory system seriously enough. As mentioned earlier, a deer's olfactory system is infinitely more sensitive than a human's.

Besides the obvious mistakes of smoking and getting smoke on his clothes from the campfire and his cigarette, the hunter misunderstood the human scent problem. Human odor is a metabolic by-product that accumulates on the body and clothes in direct proportion to the length of time since the last bath. It is a never-ending process. The more a person has sweated, the more intense his odor.

To retard the odor-producing process, the hunter should have used baking soda (bicarbonate of soda) instead of deodorant soap. Even an unscented soap would have been better. Baking soda has the ability to absorb odors and will neutralize odor for some time. It works well on clothes.

He should have rinsed his hunting clothes in soda and then put them in a plastic bag until he was ready to leave camp. This would have prevented the clothes from picking up foreign odors such as smoke and cooking smells.

Anyone camping should avoid fire and smoke on the morning of a hunt—especially if he is going to stalk, track, or take a ground stand. Smoke odors may not spook deer but they tell them that there is something unnatural in the area. That is all a cautious buck needs to go into hiding or at least stay alert.

I found out the hard way just how sensitively deer can react to foreign odors. One morning I drove directly to my hunting site after putting gas into my car. A superb buck came into the next field, about 400 yards away. I had the correct scent on, so I figured everything was in my favor as he walked toward me.

The anticipation had my heart pounding. When he got within 325 yards, it happened. The wind shifted and took my scent toward him. His head came up, he looked in my direction, then he took off as fast as he could.

As I scratched my head trying to figure out what had happened, I noticed a slight gasoline odor. Even though I had the right scent on at the time and my body and clothes were "soda" fresh, the deer picked out the gasoline odor on my hands and knew it spelled danger.

There is another good way to fight body odor: ingesting chlorophyll pills or tablets. Chlorophyll is a natural agent that greatly reduces odor. (Safariland Archery Corporation markets tablets.)

Following a few simple guidelines, we can cope with odor problems.

1. Keep your body and clothes clean—this includes your hair.
2. Remember that no miracle product will cover a 24-hour accumulation of human sweat. Not even chlorophyll.
3. Masking scents only dilute human odor and do not eliminate it.
4. Use bicarbonate of soda for bathing and rinsing your clothes when possible (or at least use non-scented soap).
5. Keep clean clothes in a plastic bag.
6. Cold camps (no fires) are best. This prevents smoke accumulation on your clothes and body.
7. If you have a pet, particularly a dog, say good-bye to your trusted friend from a distance on hunt mornings.

Having a clean body and clothes not only keeps your odor to a minimum, it also fights hypothermia (the loss of heat at a rate faster than the rate of its production by your body). I realize that when camping out in cold weather you may be hesitant to bathe and wash clothes, but failure to do so, can ruin your whole day.

Keeping clean is also something your hunting partners will appreciate. Remember, your friends can smell you long before you can smell yourself.

10

Physical Condition

Mother Nature has some hard and fast rules which everyone of us must follow like it or not. And one of these is that we must age. With every tick of the clock we get a little older. Age is something we don't feel or notice. Once we're past our late twenties it kind of creeps up on us and kicks us in the butt.

This bit of reality hit me just three seasons ago. I had just finished field-dressing a fine eight-point buck which later weighed in at 157 pounds. I was hunting alone at the time, so the business of getting the deer out of the woods was all mine.

The deer had come to rest on a steep slope just 55 yards or so from the top of the mountain. I had a choice to make. I could either drag it down the mountain and across flat land with heavy brush to a road a quarter of a mile away, or I could drag it up to the top then down the hill to an old jeep trail only about 100 yards from the top. Considering that I had taken several other deer from this same location over the years, I chose the latter route—as I had in previous years.

After securing a nylon rope around the buck's rack and snout, I tied the other end to a stout stick.

With my bow slung over my shoulder, I began to pull the deer up the mountain.

By the time I was halfway to the top I was beyond a sweat. By the time I reached the top I was well aware that the trip had never been this tough before. It wasn't because of the weight—other deer had weighed nearly as much . . . I couldn't understand it. I jog and play tennis to stay in shape, so what was the problem?

I arrived at the somewhat unsettling answer that it was age. Despite my jogging and tennis, I was not the man I had been five years before.

Off to my left and some 100 yards away was another man in much poorer condition than me. He had taken the same option and was probably arriving at the same conclusion as I. However, his being out of shape made *his* climb impossible—even with his 92 pound doe! Just yards from the top he collapsed—fortunately from exertion and not a heart attack. Later, after I had helped him back on his feet, he blamed his problem on the excitement of the hunt. He refused to admit that he was not in good physical shape, even though it was obvious.

We will never really know how many times this happens every year. Easy living has let us get soft, and vanity prevents us from admitting it.

There are some simple exercises we can do at home to keep Father Time from getting too far ahead of us. Daily exercise will help you not only in the field, but in all areas of life. You have everything to gain and nothing to lose but poor health and excess weight.

A healthy body can stay longer in a tree stand during cold weather than an unhealthy one. If that is how you hunt, then exercise will benefit you.

Beyond a doubt, the most important parts of the body for hunting—yet often the most unfit—are the legs. If you don't think so, go run up a flight of stairs two or three times. Are you breathing heavily? Could you now hold your rifle steady for a critical shot? If not, then you have a bit of work to do. Do you know why this simple exercise (running up and down stairs) causes such unstability? Because the legs require a lot of oxygen to work, and when they work hard and fast they can strip the rest of you of that oxygen. If they are exercised regularly, they become toned and carry your weight much easier— even if you are carrying an extra pound or three.

Since many of us can't find the time to exercise, we should

incorporate exercise into our daily routine. Try jogging or walking instead of riding to the neighborhood store—and do it double-time whenever possible. When you go up a flight of stairs, take two at a time. You will be using the same muscles you will use to climb the mountains and hills. And by the time hunting season rolls around you will find yourself breathing easier, which in turn will make critical shot placement easier and ensure quick, clean kills.

Arm and breathing control are important for holding a bow at full draw or keeping the crosshairs steady. For the archer, practice with a bow will sharpen his eye and tone his back and arm muscles. For the gun hunter, the most important exercises are simple pushups and chin-ups.

To get the most out of short exercise programs, exercise in slow motion. For example, the pushup should be done as follows: Push up slowly, taking three seconds or more to fully extend your arms. Hold for three seconds, then come down slowly, taking another three seconds to reach the floor. If you do this just ten times a day, your arms will be able to hold a rifle and scope steady for a long time.

Another arm exercise that will do your whole body wonders is called the "push away." After your first helping of food, simply push yourself away from the table. It will do more than just improve your hunting!

The best exercise is preseason scouting and/or small game hunting. The fresh air and the weight of outdoor clothing and hunting boots will soon let you know if you are in shape. However, if you have waited that long to decide to get into shape, it may be too late.

11

Autumn

As autumn arrives the woods offer an abundance of food. In a good mast year the nut-producing trees drop their seeds to the ground for the wildlife to feed upon. Autumn brings colors, too: the broadleaf trees decorate the countryside with an array of colors, the sweet sap trees add dabs of bright red, orange, and yellow and the bitter tannic trees add muted shades of brown.

Deer become quite active now. As acorns fall the presence of deer becomes more noticeable, and one can clearly observe their daily routine as they quickly take advantage of this rich but short-lived bounty.

Deer are more active just before dawn than after, and also in the evening. Whitetails tend to become most active after the sun has gone down.

The effect of moonlight on deer is also more noticeable now: on darker nights during the new moon you will see deer feeding earlier than usual because of the minimal light—they prefer darkness but require some light. As the phases of the moon change, deer feed later in the evening. Under a full moon, the additional light makes them nervous and they feed later and later into the evening. Many times during a full moon they do not come to the feeding area before sundown.

Instinct tells deer to store as much fat as possible before winter. They know there is little time to take advantage of the bounty, so they become compulsive eaters. Bucks, however, taper off on their eating as the rut nears.

The change of seasons also brings molting of their summer coats—exactly when depends upon various factors such as the deer's age, physical condition, subspecies, and geographic location. The short, thick summer coat which protects the deer from insects slowly changes into a thinner winter coat with long, hollow insulating guard hairs over a soft fine, kinky undercoat. As the guard hairs grow longer they take on a blueish tint—the origin of the expression "winter blue" coat.

Autumn is also the time for dispersal and migration to winter habitat. As farms and logging operations spread farther into the virgin forest, second-growth timber and brush became available for browse and cover. This ended or greatly reduced the need for long migrations to survive the winter. Today, most migrations are only a couple of miles long—compared to migrations of over 30 miles in the past. I don't mean to imply that all migration has ended. The whitetails of the northern forests (northeastern Minnesota, for example) still make long migrations. In such remote areas hunters may find no deer one day and large herds the next, as deer make their steady nightly migration. Fall migration is thought to be triggered by some combination of snow accumulation and low temperatures. If the weather should suddenly get cold, deer will head for their winter grounds and should the temperature rise only a couple of days later, the deer will head back toward the summer habitat. However, if there is considerable snow on the ground, the deer will not head back toward the summer ground.

About one third of the 1½–2½-year-old bucks which roam farm areas increase their home range from about 30 acres to about 90 acres in the fall. (In such large deer ranges as Texas, a home range may be ten times that.) A few does also disperse from their summer range of about 18 acres. Deer move from areas of high concentration and abundant food to areas of smaller populations and less food. Researchers believe that dispersal is a result of breeding competition. However it could also be nature's way of helping deer utilize all their natural resources—thus preventing natural disasters and disease from affecting an entire species.

Although young bucks disperse, they seldom leave an area altogether. Almost without fail, the buck's new area will overlap his old, especially during the rut.

12

Scents and Signals

For most game animals—particularly the white-tailed deer—the sense of smell is the key to survival. Primitive man learned through trial and error the value of masking his scent and using animal scents to attract game. He learned how to use animal oils, fats, urine, glands, dung, and hides to lure game. Wearing scent was a survival technique. Smelly, but effective.

Today commercial scents and applicators let us return to camp without stinking it up.

Experienced hunters and wildlife photographers know how important masking human odor is, and they know that the masking scent must fit in with the surroundings and, in most cases, must fit the season.

Many years ago when I had just started hunting, I was eager to learn all I could about this great sport. I spent all my spare time in the woods improving my hunting skills. One of my experiments was using the many scents that were on the market.

My tests consisted of comparing different lures of the same type (masking, sex, and food) at different times of the year. I won't win any awards for my findings, but I do believe they're worth mentioning.

Sex lures used before the buck begins making his scrapes may spook him instead of attracting him, and sex lures used more than three weeks before, or anytime after, the doe reaches estrus will spook her. They may attract a random buck, but when does spook from the untimely scent and leave the area the bucks go with them. Early-season hunters should check with local conservation officers to determine the proper time to use sexual scents.

The amount of scent also has an impact. Using too much sex scent spooks deer more often than not. You need a few drops at most every four or five hours. In wet weather you should use just a bit more to cover up the musty odor of your clothes.

Food lures will not attract deer if they are foreign to the area. When they do come to a foreign food odor, it is usually out of curiosity. Food-type lures are very effective in the winter, when food is scarce . . . but deer still approach them with great caution. (They know the scent doesn't belong there at that time of the year . . . yet cannot afford to pass up a meal.)

A third type of scent is designed to cover up human scent with that of other animals or the animal being hunted. Skunk scent is the most popular, and probably best, because skunks are common. I prefer and have had great success with fox scent, which I started using when I noticed that my fox traps were being sprung by inquisitive deer.

Putting scent on your bootsoles is a must, especially for masking or sex scents. I learned the importance of this one morning when I used the last of my lure on my camouflage clothing and didn't have enough for my bootsoles.

As I walked through the woods to my stand, I passed a primary scrape I had been watching for a couple of days. I was careful not to get too close to it as I went by. Not long after I had climbed into my stand, a young buck slowly walked out of the saplings toward the scrape. When he came to the spot where I had crossed to get to my stand, he hunched his back. The hair on his back stood straight up. He knew danger was imminent. A fast arrow stopped him before he could run, but from that day forward I have kept an extra bottle of lure with me for my boots.

Some hunters don't like to use scents on their clothes but prefer to leave it on a tree or bush some yards away. They fear that deer will follow the scent directly toward them and they won't be able to position

A few drops of scent on the soles of both shoes is a good way to keep your presence unknown and perhaps attract a deer.

themselves for a shot—or may in fact be spotted by a buck before they spot him.

Another method of using scent is to tie a piece of cotton or cloth to a string and soak it with a sex lure. After securing it to your boot, drag it through the woods behind you. This leaves a trail for bucks to follow to the hunter.

My favorite method for using a sex lure is to put a few drops in the middle of a secondary or primary scrape and on the soles of my boots. I then take a stand with a clear view some 20 yards away.

DEER SIGNALS

Whitetails use signals to communicate with their fellow deer. An outdoorsman who has learned to recognize some of the signals can accurately predict what a deer is about to do and when to make his move.

One of the most valuable signals is well known: when deer feed, they twitch their tails before raising their heads. Basically, this is true

Deer slightly alerted—note cocked leg on this button buck.

when they are feeding casually. Should you make a mistake in stalking however, their heads pop up immediately and without the tail warning. If you depend on the tail to tell you when to move, you may find yourself in a bad position and off balance for a shot.

If deer are worried, they raise and cock a front leg and flair the hair covering their tarsal glands. If their suspicions mount they stamp with their cocked leg as a warning to other deer—and perhaps too to provoke a response from whatever it is that has them worried.

If they repeat this process a few times, they are really upset. If you remain perfectly motionless, the deer may resume normal activity. If you are well camouflaged, try a few stamps of your own, imitating the deer's movement. Very often (for reasons unknown to me) the deer will relax a bit and continue to go on about their business.

However, this game might not yet be over. Very often after stamping a deer will drop his head as if to feed, then pop it up again to try and catch you making a move. He may repeat this several times, often followed by a sneeze or snort that sounds like a whistle.

Once this happens, a deer may take off for parts unknown. Sometimes they go just a short distance and slowly return, to start the fakeout maneuvers again. They don't really want to leave an area unless they are positive there is danger.

It is a sign that they intend to return if they snort and "bounce" off, stiff-legged, for a few yards then stop. The leaps they make are often over five feet high and their tails will be up. Until they have confirmed their suspicions with one of their senses, the deer most suspicious of the unknown intruder will return, often closer each time, and repeat the fakeout process. On occasions, I have seen this game last a half hour before they finally decided either to give it up or leave the area.

Any deer that walks stiff-legged and has his ears erect and cupped in one direction has been alerted by something in the area. He knows where the sound came from. His muscles are tensed like springs and he will bolt away at the slightest noise or movement. If you intend to make a move on him, wait until he has passed you or is at least looking the other way.

Frightened deer will often make high leaps with their tails up—as a warning to other deer and to provoke a response from the intruder. If other deer are present, the leaping deer will remain nearby. If not, the leaping deer will leave.

When deer bolt for cover they lay their ears back. A positive signal for you to make your move. *Photo by Leonard Lee Rue III.*

One dependable sign that deer are about to depart—especially bucks—is laid-back ears. A buck puts his delicate ears back behind his antlers and lays them along his neck for protection as he runs through the brush. Once you see his ears go back, it is time to make your move, or lose your deer.

WIND

There was over an hour and a half of daylight left when, one-by-one, the herd entered the grass field. This was their first stop on their way to a cornfield some 500 yards distant. The deer were right on time. The herd consisted of nine does and two bucks—a four-pointer and a nice eight-pointer.

In about fifteen minutes all were in range except the bucks, who lagged behind because they were sparring in the middle of the field. The bigger eight-pointer had little trouble shoving the smaller buck around.

Soon they too were moving in my direction. Things looked promising as they came within 50 yards. Then a wandering hunter came through the woods to get to his stand. The deer retreated, leaving the field the same way they entered. After 30 minutes the deer again entered the field enroute to the cornfield, and again they were disturbed—this time by a Doberman pinscher and a mutt from a neighboring farmhouse.

Just 20 minutes later, they could be seen cutting across the lower end of the field, inside the corner, as they headed for their intended feeding area.

From what I could gather, they picked their ultimate destination by the wind: whenever the wind blew from the lower cornfield, they would head that way and would not be sidetracked. When the wind

The laid-back ear position on most of these deer indicates that they are nervous and will cross the field with little delay.

Tails clamped down on running bucks. Buck deer will often run with their tails clamped down so they can blend in with their surrounding cover, even if they are not yet in cover. *Photo by Leonard Lee Rue III.*

came from another direction, the deer would seek the field in that direction.

By realizing that their strong dependence on their sense of smell greatly determines which trail deer will use, you can plan your moves. Even if deer are spooked while moving toward you, you can predict their route. Just move closer to their intended field or feeding area. After detouring around danger, they will head into the wind for feeding or bedding.

13

Calling Deer

One of the most exciting ways to bag a deer is by calling him to you. Unfortunately, too many hunters aren't willing to spend enough time in the woods to learn this fascinating art. They purchase a call, try it a few times, and give up if they don't attract a deer. This is sad, because a deer call, when used right, is one of the best ways to bag a deer.

A call works best where the deer population is high and hunting pressure light. In the early season all deer—and bucks near time of the rut—respond well. Even if you only attract does, that's alright, because, as the rut nears, bucks go where does do.

Patience pays.

The Alaskan deer call is the one I am most familiar with and have used for over 15 years with great success. It is made of two flat pieces of plastic secured by a rubber band. When blown, the rubber band vibrates and makes the sound of a bleating deer, or, if blown hard, the warning blow of the alarmed deer. I have found that the soft calls imitating the "ba-a-a" sound of a fawn work well. I start out blowing just loud enough for a hunter 100 yards away to hear. I make three or four calls, then stop for about 15 minutes. I repeat this at lower volume. After remaining silent for another 15 minutes I make a couple more bleats—these soft and quivering, as though the fawn was hurt.

If I don't get a response within 20 minutes, I move on a couple hundred yards and start over.

The Burnham Brothers produce several types of deer call, including one designed for long range. This model (D-4) must be blown hard the first half dozen or so times. After waiting a few minutes, the volume is reduced as with the other kind.

Whichever call you use be sure to call no longer than one or two seconds at a time. As you reduce the volume you should be doing more looking than calling, because deer will approach very cautiously. Don't expect an answer to your call either: I have had only two does actually bleat back in twenty years of calling. A curious deer circles before coming close to inspect, so keep your eyes peeled. If you spot him, don't attempt to call him in any closer, as you will probably spook him. Let him search for you.

Mouth-blown calls have a few qualities I find extremely valuable. I have used them to literally stop a deer in his tracks for a clean shot. When they hear that sound they stop and listen. When they locate the source, you had better be camouflaged or remain motionless, because they are alert to the slightest movement.

If you spot a deer wandering away from you in a thicket, give the call a slightly louder blow. That usually causes a deer to stop and raise his head high. With a gun, that's all you need. A short, loud whistle will often suffice in this instance.

When approaching a field full of deer, you can really appreciate a call's usefulness. Here you can witness the reactions to your call—and calm them down if you have startled them with a too-loud approach. If you have caught their attention while making your stalk, give a couple soft bleats on the call and you will fool them into thinking it is an approaching fawn.

I have found that, although deer respond to calls throughout the day, the best time to use them is early morning and evening. With blown calls it is best to be in a tree stand—or at least to have another hunter to help watch for approaching deer.

In the Northeast, where rolling hills and thick brush muffle much of the sound that is made, and hunting pressure is quite heavy, the tactic of calling doesn't seem to work quite so well. In my home state of New Jersey, my success has largely been limited to calling other deer hunters in the immediate area.

RATTLING BUCKS

Rattling antlers is a highly successful method of calling whitetails, especially in the southwestern part of the country. This must be done during or near the rut, and the area should have definite signs of several bucks—the more the better, because this adds to the competition among rutting bucks. An indication of the number of bucks in the area is the number of rubs and scrapes. If they are quite common in an area of 300 or so acres, rattling should work quite well.

Once you pick an area, you should take a stand as early in the morning as possible. The crack of dawn is the best time for rattling. Sundown is also good. If possible, you should have the rising sun at your back and not be on the crest of a hill. After making yourself comfortable, make sure you have a clear shot at any deer coming from downwind of you. That is the direction a buck will most likely come from.

Use a pair of heavily-beamed, uniformly-sized antlers which have been sawed off at the base. They should have at least four points per side and have long tines. Heavy beams and long tines vibrate better, giving a more realistic sound. Before going afield, remove the eyeguard tines. The eyeguards get in the way and can injure your hands.

Grip the antlers and clash them together firmly. Rattle the tines against each other. Do this two or three times over a 10- or 15-minute period, while raking the ground and brush to simulate a real fight.

It is hard to say just how bucks will respond to rattling. Some will come at you in a rush as if to defend their area or steal does away from battling bucks. Or, they may sneak in out of curiosity.

In the northeast, where rolling hills and thick brush muffle the sound and hunting pressure is heavy, rattling doesn't seem to work as well—especially for firearms hunters. Bow hunters, however, seem to do better because there are fewer hunters to spook the deer.

If you are successful in rattling up a buck, you can make him come closer by very gently clicking the tines together. As in calling with a mouth-blown call, it helps to have a friend along to spot deer. Rattling should be done on the ground—for some reason rattling antlers up in a tree just doesn't sound natural.

14

Hunting Methods: Stalking and Driving

There are four ways to hunt whitetail: stalking/tracking, driving, stillhunting, and hunting from a stand. Depending on the quarry, the terrain, the weather, and the number of other hunters in the area, each has its advantages and disadvantages. Whatever the method, hunters who take the time to polish their skills more fully appreciate hunting as a sport and are successful year after year.

STALKING

Stalking is probably the hardest hunting skill to master. It requires a great deal of patience, self-control, and practice.

The odds are against the stalker right from the start. He has big clumsy feet, and stands vertically (no other animal on our continent does this). He has an unmistakable odor, and he is in the backyard of an animal that has senses far superior to his own.

On the other side of the coin, we have a brain capable of logic and a means of reaching out at great distances to kill or capture on film. So, theoretically, we are even. Right? Well, if so, why are so many hunters unsuccessful at stalking?

I believe the answer is lack of patience and self-control.

Every year I watch hunter after hunter try to stalk or track white-tails and I always see them make one major mistake: they move through the woods too fast. Almost without fail, a hunter will travel 50 or more yards in less than 5 minutes. That's alright if you are following a fresh set of tracks which indicate the deer is moving that fast. In fact, you have to move as he moves to keep up with him for a shot. But even then, the hunter should try to remember that the quarry is just as likely to be behind the next tree or bush as he is to be miles away.

The point to remember in hunting is that it is 80-percent vision, 10-percent hearing, and only 10-percent legwork. In all kinds of hunting, only the hunter that will spot the quarry before the quarry spots him will be successful. So as a rule, if you want to sneak up on an animal you should take at least 20 minutes to travel 100 yards, and preferably a half hour. If you have trouble moving that slowly, you can learn: Simply relax and enjoy the beauty around you. If you are tense and excited you move too fast and skip over important details. If your eyes move slowly, chances are that your feet will too.

Footwear is important for stalking whitetails. You should be able to feel the ground as you carefully place your feet down. I prefer well-broken-in boots or, weather permitting, sneakers. Heavy rubber or plastic soles of the cleat design are unfavorable for stalking unless there is snow or a lot of loose rocks are on the ground. These soles seem to give little feel and pick up small sticks and twigs and drag them through the leaves. Obviously, one does not want this to happen while stalking.

Almost every stalker has a particular style or method he uses to make his way quietly through the forest. All agree, though, that the best procedure—unless following a specific set of tracks—is to pick a trail which offers the fewest dead branches or blowdowns, thorns, and large puddles of water. Whenever possible use well-traveled trails, where obstructions have been removed by the animal you seek.

Many stalkers move from tree to tree to keep their images broken and to have something to hide behind should they spot game.

Most stalkers and trackers find that the quietest way to walk through the woods is to pick their feet directly up from the ground and place them down again, either heel or toe first, rather than dragging them along. Most find it easier to step heel-first on dirt or grass surfaces and toe-first on rocky terrain. In either case, they always use half-steps, so that they are always in balance and ready to freeze if their prey is suddenly looking at them. Half-steps also allow them to feel the ground and quietly break the small twigs beneath their feet as they transfer their weight from one foot to another.

With each small and carefully placed step, the stalker should scan each and every bush and tree for a glimpse of the quarry. Remember, every step taken offers a totally new view of the area. You will seldom get a full view of an animal in a forest or fields, especially in the early season. Look for anything horizontal, or blotches in a brush patch, bush, or between trees. Squat every now and then to look under the brush: the view is better at a low angle, and you will see leg movements.

Probably the biggest mistake a stalker makes is to neglect to keep his silhouette broken up at all times. This is not a mistake to make when hunting deer or antelope. Always remember to stay close to trees or brush. Stay off the crests of hills. If you have to cross a hilltop or crest, do it very slowly and crouch low if no cover is available. The reason I advise moving slowly while at the crest of a hill instead of quickly, as others often recommend, is that quick movement is easily noticed whereas slow movement is not. Keep the sun at your back, or at least stay in the shadows. Even the sharpest eyes have trouble with sharp lighting contrasts and blinding sun.

An important point to remember when stalking deer is that animals expect danger from behind them. They will constantly stop and check behind them for long periods of time. For this reason, I have found it easiest to get close by stalking crosswind rather than upwind.

Also, when tracking or stalking, remember that the quarry will cross open areas to make any predator that may be following expose himself. If when tracking an animal you approach a clearing or thinly covered area, stop before you reach the edge and study the other side. If possible, remain in thick brush or woods and make a wide circle around to the other side to cut off your quarry before he continues on. You may even catch him waiting for you at the edge.

In areas of thin or spotty cover, it is also wise—once you have determined the direction in which the animal is heading—to follow at least 50 yards to the side of the trail. Keep your eyes peeled for movement about 100 yards ahead of the quarry's trail. Because man is not one of the quietest animals in the woods, it is rare that a whitetail isn't aware of him by the time he is within 30 yards. Even if you aren't on a fresh track but are just stalking, it is good practice to keep your eyes searching the distant brush as well as what is immediately in front of you.

The weather plays a primary role in deciding where and when to stalk. One of the best times to stalk is during or just after a rain, when the forest floor is almost as quiet as a carpet. Water makes leaves and small twigs very pliable, and even the unavoidable noise you make as you move through brush is muffled. Also, your scent doesn't carry as far in damp weather. This alone is a great advantage because it allows you more freedom in your approach. At distances of 100 yards or more you can take the chance of letting your scent be carried, momentarily, in the direction of your quarry.

A heavy snowfall, or a cold snap after a snowfall, makes a quiet stalk nearly impossible. The exception to this is in heavy cedar stands. Here you will find yourself bending down most of the time in order to be able to see any movement at all. If you have a weak back don't attempt it.

A breezy day is another good time to try tracking and stalking. If you move when the wind rustles the leaves on the forest floor, deer find it hard to distinguish between the natural rustling and your occasionally noisy approach. However, animals are a bit more edgy on a windy day and you will find they spook at the slightest unnatural movement. Therefore you must travel slowly with your eyes peeled for any glimpse of your quarry. Such areas as cedar and pine stands are ideal for stalking in windy weather. On windy wintery days you will find deer on the lee side of mountains and in ravines, hollows, and swamps.

Even under the best conditions, you must contend with still another vital element: your quarry's fellow creatures. The squirrel and blue jay are two of nature's watch-dogs which have spoiled even the best tracking efforts.

Inhabitants of the forests seem to understand what their fellow creatures say or do. Because they are familiar with each other's natural movements and sounds, an alarm sound by one draws the attention of all.

This does not necessarily send deer into flight. I have never seen or heard of that happening. A sudden outburst or alarm will often catch a deer's attention however, if only momentarily, and if you are careless at that instant, the deer may spot you. It is to your benefit to pay attention to all the creatures as you move through the woods—besides, they are fun to watch!

Stalking on dry leaves on a quiet day will give serious hunters ulcers—especially bowhunters and photographers. I've tried putting heavy socks over my boots, or wearing sneakers to muffle the crunchy sound, but the results have been less than spectacular. I have found that shuffling my feet through the leaves to imitate a squirrel, or a buck as he plods through the leaves when in rut, to be the best approach. Trying to be too quiet under these circumstances is not only nearly impossible, it is unnatural. If you don't blend in with the environment, your chance of success drops very sharply.

Should you be spotted by your quarry when you can't get off a shot, freeze. The animal may decide you are not a threat and resume his business or move slowly away. This happens most often to the hunter or photographer wearing camouflage. Their broken image, although a concern to the animal, will often delay departure, and that may be all you need.

If the animal remains, but shows signs of nervousness, or appears to be upset by your presence, you can do one of three things:

Move slowly away from him and get out of sight as soon as possible. If he feels you have left the area, he may offer you another chance at a stalk.

Another choice is often made by hunters and photographers when there is little or no cover: the meandering approach. This works best when the animal has the chance to observe you from a distance. The object here is to stay in view of the animal during the entire stalk. Your movements should be slow, but not sneaky: you cannot appear to be stalking him. Look elsewhere as you head in his direction. If the animal appears nervous, sit down and relax for a while until you feel he has also relaxed. As they get closer, some photographers and hunters quietly talk to the animal. It seems to relax them. You have probably tried this with such other animals as horses, dogs, etc.. This method works best on such animals as wild goats and sheep because they seldom if ever see humans. Obviously, this would never work on mature deer in heavily-hunted areas. They are too familiar with man and the danger he represents.

The third choice is to wait him out. When he turns his head, make your move.

TRACKING TIPS

A fresh set of tracks has sharp edges. Older tracks have rounded edges because wind, rain, and dew have eroded them. The sides of fresh tracks will be damp and not crusty.

Sometimes dirt particles kicked out of the tracks will land nearby. If the particles are darker in color (damper) than the surrounding ground, the tracks are fairly fresh.

In marshy or wet ground, look for water filtering into the tracks. If it is just starting, the tracks have obviously been made recently.

Take note of any special characteristics or deformities that the tracks may have. Also note if footprints are spread out at the tips and if there are dew-claw impressions (on tracks of any split-hoofed animal, especially whitetails). This helps determine the animal's pace and the pace you will have to keep to catch him.

If the ground is firm, and hoofprints are spread at the tips and headed in a fairly straight direction, the quarry is in a hurry and traveling at a fast pace. Be careful here. Some people don't pay attention to the condition of the ground and misread the tracks because of soft ground. Soft, muddy ground, or even dry sandy ground, will spread the hoofprint and cause dew-claw marks even if the animal was walking.

A more accurate way to tell how fast a deer is traveling is to note the distance between the sets of tracks. This may require tracks on a clear section of ground, so that they are not mixed up with others. If the sets of prints are more than 21 inches apart, he is picking up his pace. The normal distance between sets is 17–19 inches. If the sets are more than two feet apart, he is moving along at a trot. If the print sets are six feet or more apart, he is running.

Note that a running whitetail print will show the hind hoofprint (the one with the dew claws farther away from the toe) *in front of* the front hoofprint. This is because the whitetail has a rocking, or scissor-like gait, as do all other four-legged big game animals—except mule deer.

Mule deer have a bounding gait that leaves all four prints close together, with the front hoofprints in front and the hind prints in back. When hunting in an area where both whitetail and mule deer abound, this may be the only way to tell their tracks apart.

Check the pattern of travel as you follow along. If the gait is slow

Whitetail deer run with a scissor-like gait.

and the tracks a little erratic in pattern (little or no distinct direction), the deer may be browsing or getting ready to bed down. If the gait is fairly slow and much more direct, with very little meandering, this is a good indication that the tracks belong to a nice buck—perhaps on the trail of a doe.

Before going on to *driving* I want to say a word about determining a deer's sex from its tracks. I haven't yet met a person who can accurately tell a deer's sex from its hoofprints alone, even though some people insist they can.

Some claim they can determine sex by the presence of dew-claw marks left in snow or soft ground. This supposedly indicates the track is of a buck. But I've watched too many does make the same type of print to swallow this theory.

Others claim that bucks walk in a more direct fashion, whereas does meander along a trail. During the rut, this is often true. It is also claimed that bucks drag their hooves, leaving drag marks in leaves and on powdery snow.

I've also heard that bucks walk with their toes pointed outward.

Many say that the biggest tracks are a buck's, but I can't go along with this. In heavily-hunted areas bucks don't often get to full maturity, and dominant does may be larger. In areas with less-than-desirable deer management programs, laws may restrict harvesting does. In "buck only" areas you find huge does.

Some claim the hoofprints on buck tracks are more rounded than on those of does. They say this because they believe bucks wear down their points pawing the ground to make scrapes. But if the advocates of this theory had spent a bit more time in the woods they would have found that does also paw the ground, especially in the winter, to search for food. I have found that roundness does correlate to age however: an older animal has put a lot of miles on his hooves, which obviously has rounded them off.

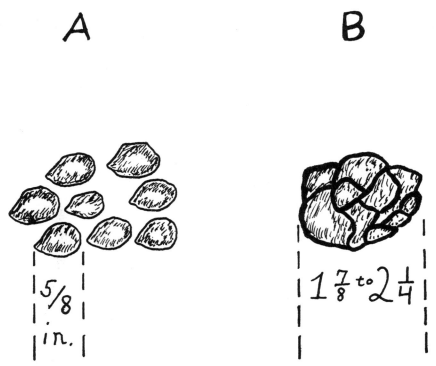

A. Segmented droppings are the type most commonly found, especially from fall through spring. *B*. During the summer, droppings are very often in a mass instead of in segments. Fresh droppings of either type will have a wet appearance and be warm and soft. In warm weather, flies will be present within minutes of the droppings having been left.

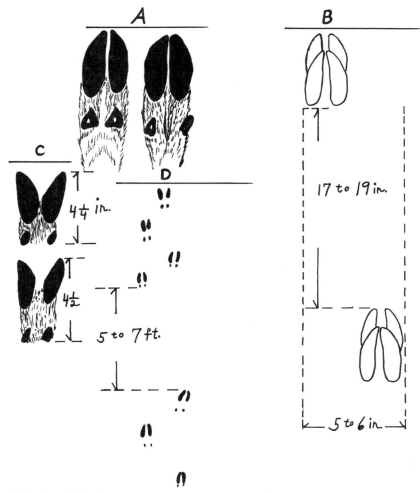

A. Hoof on left is a front hoof. Hoof on right is a hind hoof.

B. A track inside of a track indicates a walking deer. The 17- to 19-inch span between tracks is the average distance between sets of tracks on a full-grown deer. A fawn or small deer will have a span of only about 12 to 14 inches. If the tracks are headed in a generally straight direction, the deer is headed for a specific destination, usually cover. If the tracks meander, it indicates that the deer has been feeding or browsing.

C. Splayed tracks left on soft ground by a leaping deer. Top track is of the front hoof (dewclaws are close to hoof). Bottom track shows hind hoof (dewclaws are farther back).

D. Tracks of a galloping deer will show the hind hoofs ahead of the front hoofs and the track sets will usually be between five and seven feet apart. A tracker can pick up his pace if following this kind of track.

During the rut I lean toward a combination of some of these claims as a general guide for tracking. I look for tracks which are large, dragging, slightly-pointed-outward, and indicate little meandering.

This combination has worked very well.

There are other reliable ways to determine if you are following a buck or doe. In snow, you can tell by the urine. A buck leaves a dribbling trail a few inches or even a foot long; a doe will not do that.

During and just before the rut, look for nose and antler marks in the snow. When trailing a doe, a buck periodically puts his nose into the tracks of another deer to see if it is a doe in estrus. In doing so he will leave antler marks in the snow, especially if he has a large rack.

DRIVING

Driving is one of the most productive ways to harvest deer or any other large big-game animal. Driving is often a controversial subject among sportsmen—especially when dogs are used.

The success of a drive depends on how well you use the terrain and how well you know your quarry's habits.

The box or gang drive. My first deer hunts were drives in the New Jersey pinelands. We used the box drive. In the pinelands, this method is simple because the land is flat and the woods are broken up into convenient sections by numerous roads and fire cuts. From the air, it looks like a checker-board.

The object was to gather as many men as possible and surround one of the sections. When the box was complete, half the men (the drivers) walked toward the other half making loud noises. The captains of each team were chosen for their knowledge of the area. Usually they had portable communications radios (walkie-talkies) to coordinate the drive and to discuss any problems that might occur. The men on the flanks either joined the drivers, kept ahead of them, or fell behind to take any deer that broke through undetected.

The drivers were about 30 yards apart (we used shotguns). This naturally varied with the density of the brush we would be going through. The important point here was that the drivers were able to see each other as well as anything that got between them. This was supposed to prevent deer from doubling back through the drive line as it proceeded toward the standers.

The drivers formed and maintained a straight line from one end to the other. Very often one or two men would run into difficulty in thick brush and when this happened, the line would be halted and reformed.

This method often required some very fast shooting near the end of the drive, when the deer would know they were confined and would tend to panic. After deciding which way they wanted to run, they would usually run through the drivers and standers at full speed—about 35–40 miles per hour.

Some deer came out very fast and very low to the ground. I still can't figure out how they traveled so fast in such an awkward position! However, even in a noisy drive, whitetails rely on stealth instead of speed.

In one instance, during a noisy drive in the pinelands, I was looking slightly downhill toward the drivers, who were only 100 yards away and closing. I had seen a few does wandering off to the side, getting ready to break through the drive—but had seen no sign of a buck. As the drivers came closer, I watched the man directly in front of me weave through the brush yelling "Yo-buck!" He was near the edge of the woods when he stepped over a heavy log and right onto the back of a buck! Startled, he nearly fell over and did not get a shot off. The buck had apparently been there during the entire drive—probably since we took our stand position. If he hadn't been stepped on he probably would not have moved at all!

At the completion of the drive, the gang went from one section to another. If that particular area proved unproductive, they hopped into their vehicles and headed for another area.

Since the drive was well-organized and the men close together, you may think the deer had very little chance of escape. Not so. Conservation officials in various states have proven this. In one test officials attached a radio transmitter to a brightly colored collar—in another test they tied bright streamers to the antlers—and released the buck so marked into a confined area. Then they staged a drive. Time after time, men would pass within yards of the hidden deer without spotting him. The test also showed the men being outmaneuvered. Also, many hunters are "deer blind," and do not practice enough with their weapons to be able to hit a fast-moving target.

You can see that the odds, even when a box drive is on, are nearly even.

The silent drive. If you don't have enough men to make a box drive, then you must know deer habits well. You must know bedding areas, feeding areas, and the major trails leading to and from them. You must also keep in mind that deer are not driven but simply moved around in this kind of drive.

You will find that you should be very quiet and that your drive will be more productive if you keep it as short as possible—½ mile or less is best. The longer the drive, the smaller the chances of moving deer toward the standers, because they can break out to the side or circle the drivers with ease.

A silent drive offers the drivers a chance to hear deer as they move ahead of them. A silent drive doesn't spook deer into a dead run.

As in all hunting and wildlife photography, the wind factor should be kept in mind. If there is a breeze, drive crosswind or downwind so deer move at moderate speed when they go past the standers. The drivers' scent won't panic them, but it keeps them moving at a steady pace. It also masks the standers' presence.

I prefer to drive crosswind because it helps keep the drivers hidden longer—or at least unknown long enough to give them a good shot at a buck cutting back through the drive.

Standers should stay on well-used trails between bedding and feeding areas. If the deer have been driven for two or more days, standers should stay on escape routes: trails that lead from one patch of ground or thick section of woods to another. Standers should also stay either crosswind or downwind from the deer, and should pick their stands quickly and conceal themselves as best they can, preferably above a trail which they feel will produce deer.

If the area is narrow enough, use flankers (men at the sides of the drive). They will take many deer on farmland or where deer have several optional escape routes.

Always set up the drive so that you funnel the deer toward the standers. Drive from the widest to the narrowest part of the woods. The reason for this is that near the end of the drive the limited habitat will make the deer nervous and they will make their move. A tight funnel will give them less chance to outmaneuver you.

Terrain can help you do this, since deer do not like to cross open fields for great distances when man is present. Choose smaller patches, "islands" of ground, and place standers at the narrowest places or between patches of woods.

Steep ridges and fast, deep water on one or both sides of a woods help confine deer, or at least urge them to head in a specific direction.

In the mornings, you should try to cover the lowlands and valleys. Orchards and cornfields are other good places to start a drive. As the day progresses, you should drive higher ground. At midday, try areas where thick cover offers deer considerable security from intruders.

One of my favorite places to drive is a deep, wooded ravine bordered by open ridges. Here bucks tend to hold to the cover the ravine offers and head for an escape route near the top. The standers set up where the wind won't betray them and where they can get off a clear shot.

If the ravine is not bordered on both sides with open ridges, locate one or two men near any cover leading out of the ravine.

The pivot drive.   Sometimes the terrain dictates a pivot drive. Here the drivers form a line extending from a pivot man located at the narrow part of the woods or the high point in the area. If there is wind, the pivot man should be either crosswind or downwind of the deer.

The drivers on the end of the line should be men or boys in good shape, because they do most of the walking. They start first and walk around the contour of the land toward the standers, or toward the sheer cliffs of whatever is used to block the deer from running off. They "funnel" the deer toward the pivot man, so anyone in the crew may get a shot as the deer are pushed toward the pivot.

This kind of drive can be used in place of a line drive to confuse the deer. It works well where deer are quite accustomed to line drives. Under these circumstances, the deer stay just ahead of the drivers instead of trying to break through. On a pivot drive, the pivot man will usually get a shot at a slow-moving deer which stops to figure out the new situation.

Whichever way you decide to put on your drive, you should always set up as quickly and quietly as possible. Because deer cannot count, it is sound practice for each driver and stander to take his position quickly and remain still.

I took my first buck, a small eight-pointer, only seconds after I

The Ravine Drive: Natural land configurations help direct the deer toward the top of the ravine, where the deer have escape routes. Note that the standers position themselves *above* the deer.

WIND

The Pivot Drive: Use natural borders such as fields, fast rivers, or sheer cliffs to set up this drive.

was dropped off at a stand position. I was a stander, and was the second man in from a road. I immediately took a position under a pine tree and was settled before the rest of the team passed by down a fire path to set up the box pattern. The group had gone just 50 yards down the path and dropped off the next man when a buck got up out of the brush just 30 yards behind me.

Thinking that all the intruders had gone away and that the danger had passed, he slowly walked across the path and passed in front of me. When he stopped to check the location of the men again, I had an easy ten-yard shot.

When deer break through a drive, don't give up. They usually remain in the general area and sometimes in the section of woods that

The Zig-Zag Drive: The driver should walk at a medium pace to confuse the deer. With this pattern the deer aren't sure if you are coming or going, and may keep just ahead of the driver for a while before trying to circle.

The Staggered, or Drop-Out Drive: The second man should be as quiet as possible and the lead man should make only slight noises to make his presence barely known.

you just finished driving. Check the perimeter for fresh tracks to see where they went and set up immediately. I've driven a piece of woods three times before getting the one buck I knew was in there.

The two man drive.   If you have only two or three men, your drive must be very short, about 200–300 yards, to enable the stander to cover the entire area. Funnels that lead to a hedgerow or to an adjoining patch of woods are key areas. Other good places are bottlenecks in a narrow stretch of woods and entrances to swamps or cedar stands.

The zig-zag drive.   The driver has several options when making his drive. One of my favorites is the zig-zag pattern. Here, after giving the stander time to get set, the driver makes a large zig-zag pattern as he slowly heads in the general direction of the stander. The driver should be walking with the wind at his back or crosswind.

The staggered drive.   A very effective tactic for two men, or a small group, is to have one driver walk about 100 yards behind the other to catch circling deer. This is a good method when working toward a stander or when you and your friends wish to head for another location. If a stander is not used, walk into the wind or crosswind.

The circle drive.   Another very effective method for two men is to have one slowly walk in large circles, while making a complete circle around the stander. This keeps the deer completely confused and off guard. The stander must be careful when he shoots because he cannot

The Circle Drive: During the circle drive the stander will benefit if he positions himself on a rise or some other high point.

be completely sure where the driver is. This drive works best if the stander is located on a rise or other form of elevation.

The mountain drive.   A fourth method is to place one man on top of a hill and have the other walk through the thickets at the bottom. When spooked at the bottom of the hill, deer usually cross over the top to the other side rather than run around the hill. When on top, deer

The Mountain Drive: This drive is best done between mid-morning and mid-afternoon. The driver should walk, making a little noise from time to time.

usually stop to check on the intruder at the bottom before continuing to the other side. If the stander is alert, he will have an easy shot.

The parallel drive. The parallel drive is another effective drive that can be made with just two men. In this drive pattern the men should be parallel to each other during the drive and from 75–100 yards apart. The men should be walking into the wind or crosswind. Deer spooked by one man will either try to sneak around him or will run ahead, then try to circle behind.

15

Hunting Methods: Stillhunting and Stand Hunting

Stillhunting can be defined as the art of letting the animal find you. Stalking quietly is also known as stillhunting to some people, because a stalker must stop moving from time to time to watch game trails, ridgetops, or other areas that the quarry may pass in his daily travels. Standing while other hunters pass you by and waiting for circling game to come into view is also stillhunting. The best definition of stillhunting is a combination of stalking and stand hunting.

Stillhunting fits the nature of most hunters I know. Not everyone can sit or stand motionless in a blind or tree stand for several hours, nor can many people take the physical punishment of driving deer through thick brush all day.

One of the most effective methods of stillhunting, especially in unfamiliar territory, is to make large circular patterns through the area as you alternately stalk and take stands. When taking stands in this manner, you should remain at each location for at least half an hour before moving on.

This leads us to the next method, one of the most popular and effective ways to hunt: stand hunting.

Stand hunting is the best way to hunt big game—particularly whitetails—because virtually everything is in the hunter's favor. Stand hunters do not have to match their senses against the superior senses of wild game, and they aren't likely to make very much noise or movement. The stand hunter also has the advantage of controling his scent by choosing which side of the trail to wait on. Because his presence is unknown to the quarry, he usually gets a slow-moving or standing target.

Choosing a stand is often hard for many hunters. With so many variables to consider—especially in a good area—many hunters choose a stand on intuition and count on Lady Luck to do the rest. I whole-heartedly believe in luck, but luck is most often made by careful planning and preseason scouting.

PRESEASON SCOUTING

Because scouting is such a vital factor in locating a good area to place a stand, it must precede any decisions. You must know as much as possible about whitetails—and about the herd in your area.

Local wildlife changes from year to year and season to season. Scouting done two months in advance may indicate a heavy population or a spectacular trophy, but when you return on opening day, you may not find a trace of deer. As the weather or the browse changes, animals make necessary adjustments. For instance, local crops—either natural or agricultural—that the deer feed on may have been depleted or harvested. Animals must then seek new browse in other areas. It's a natural fact: when the food is gone, so are the animals.

When you look for signs in the woods, keep in mind that a few deer can make a lot of tracks. Don't concern yourself with the number of tracks—unless they are fresh. The best way to find fresh tracks is to look for them just after a rain or snow. If that is not possible, you can use the thread method: tie a length of thread from bush to bush across a well-used trail in the morning and check it again in the after-noon. If it is broken or torn from the bush, a deer or other large animal has passed. Check the ground for tracks. Note the direction of travel: if the string is broken in the morning it indicates the direction of the bedding area. If broken during the late afternoon or before dawn it indicates that the animal is headed for a feeding area. Again, check the prints for the direction.

Bottlenecks joining two or more sections of woods are key areas for stands. Several emergency trails as well as regular trails will be found here.

Note, too, that there are two types of trails. The normal "runs" are well-traveled and usually lead to and from bedding and feeding areas. The others are escape routes.

Because whitetails are not great travelers, bedding areas are not usually very far from feeding areas. You can trace a well-used run to both areas and mark the places you feel will offer you the best chance.

In heavily-hunted areas, you should try to locate the emergency runs because when hunters invade the area, deer will use them most frequently. They will be located in and through areas of heavy brush leading from one section of woods to another. I will elaborate on this in HUNTING THE HEAVILY HUNTED AREAS.

As I mentioned earlier, trails and tracks won't tell you the sex of the animal, so it is important to look for details along the way. Try to locate rubs or scrapes because they will tell you that a buck is in

In the early morning, and especially in the evening, deer will often visit fields. With a little patience, a stand at any of the marked areas (X) will pay off.

the area. Right before the rut, locate at least one large scrape and take a stand near it.

As you search for good trails you will find that the most heavily used trails are in the "fringe" areas between feeding areas and deep forest. Fringe areas offer heavy cover and browse, and while in these areas deer usually proceed slowly. They do not stay long, however, because they want to get into more open feeding and bedding areas where they can utilize their sharp senses fully.

Travels from bedding to feeding areas have a definite pattern. Deer move from open fields and less-wooded areas at or around dawn to densely-wooded areas for bedding and protection. At evening, the process is reversed.

If you are in unfamiliar territory looking for a place to start scouting, a map will show you the lay of the land. You should limit your search to places that appear to be fringe areas: patches of woods, draws, swamp edges, and ridgetops. Other good locations indicated on most maps are fire lanes, feeding areas developed by the conservation department, and woods bordering farm areas.

If you take your time scouting an area, you may be fortunate enough to catch a glimpse of a fine buck. For this reason, it is a good idea to carry a camera with a 400-mm telephoto lens and a roll of high speed black and white film. This will let you take a fine photograph at a distance without spooking the animal. High speed film is a plus in the early season when foliage limits light or at evening and early dawn when lighting is poor.

If you spot a fine specimen, try to return to the place where you saw him a few more times before the season opens. If you see the same buck where he was before, you have discovered a vital pattern of his movement and increased your chances dramatically.

Also note the time you see the animals, the trail they use, wind direction, and the direction in which they head. This tells you when these creatures of habit will come through the area, and whether they are going to feed or bed. The wind and trail notation will tell you which trail the deer will probably use when the wind blows from that direction again. The direction noted indicates where they prefer to feed and where their bedding areas may be.

Take note of any special characteristics the deer may have. Once you spot unique details on one of them, you can develop a mental picture and a feel for the natural pattern of the herd and identify them if you spot them again. This is important to know when choosing your stand.

Topographical maps—or even handmade maps—are valuable tools, especially when spotting your quarry and writing down facts about them, and can often pinpoint the best stand for you.

The value of this method became apparent to me several years ago when I spotted a fine buck early in the archery season. I had seen him several times, but unfortunately, every time he appeared he was just out of range. I was beginning to get a little frustrated. It seemed as though he never took the same trail twice, but I knew better than that. *Every* buck has a pattern of his own, and a spot he crosses at least once every other day, if not every day, especially as the rut approaches. My problem was finding *this* buck's pattern. With only a week left in the season, I had to locate it fast.

After breakfast one morning, I grabbed a pencil and paper and made a map of the area. On it I made marks every place I had spotted him. I marked down the direction he came from and headed to, the time of the day, the wind direction, and every rub or scrape I knew.

After I had everything marked down, I began to draw lines across the paper. Using this method, I not only located his center of activity, I was able to arrive at the approximate time he would appear in that area. If not disturbed by other hunters in the area, he should appear on schedule.

At 10:30 the next morning I was sitting high—in the most uncomfortable tree you could imagine—taking aim at him. His rack is now a permanent fixture in my house.

HUNTING BEDDING AREAS

Once you pick an area to hunt, locate a spot for the stand itself. The most effective place to set up an ambush is about halfway between the main feeding area and the bedding area. Deer will pass through at least twice a day as they head to and from their feeding and bedding spots. Another benefit is shooting time: deer will pass through while there is plenty of light. Still another advantage is tracking time: if a hunter makes a hit near an evening feeding area, he may lose the deer while tracking in the dim light.

Deer travel less cautiously on these trails than near bedding or main feeding areas. They also browse on their way, which distracts them.

With all these advantages it is understandable that so many hunters put in a lot of time locating the trails leading to the center of a herd's home area—or "core"—where the deer bed. The core area, by the way, is maybe as small as 10 acres or as large as 25 depending upon the available food and the terrain.

The best way to locate core or bedding areas is to first locate the main night feeding areas. These are usually quite easily located. Deer favor open fields, burnt patches of woods with plenty of new growth, abandoned farms, old or new orchards, and fields of anything from corn to clover.

When investigating these areas, check to see that they have both old and new sign. This combination will indicate that the area is used repeatedly. Just old or just new sign indicates only that a random deer has passed through the area. Once you locate a well-used feeding area, locate at least one more. When you locate the next one or two, find the most used trails leading into and out of the area. Follow each of these trails toward the woods. When doing so, pay close attention to trail intersections. You may find other main trails leading to and from the feeding areas to the core or bedding areas. These intersections indicate that you have found a main trail and you should consider placing a stand at that location.

When I locate such areas I try to move closer to the bedding areas, though. There I not only get to see and study a herd, I may get to see members of other herds as they cross the core area.

WIND

Wind is probably the most important factor to consider when choosing the site of your stand. Unless deer are pushed, they follow basic instincts and travel upwind so they can scent danger ahead of them. Because the wind changes from day to day, deer have alternate trails to get to bedding and feeding locations. When you decide which trail to hunt, be sure always to stand downwind from it. Take notice of the prevailing winds *and* the thermal currents, which move vertically.

As the morning sun warms the ground, the air rises. This air current flows up the sides of hills or mountains until it cools. In the

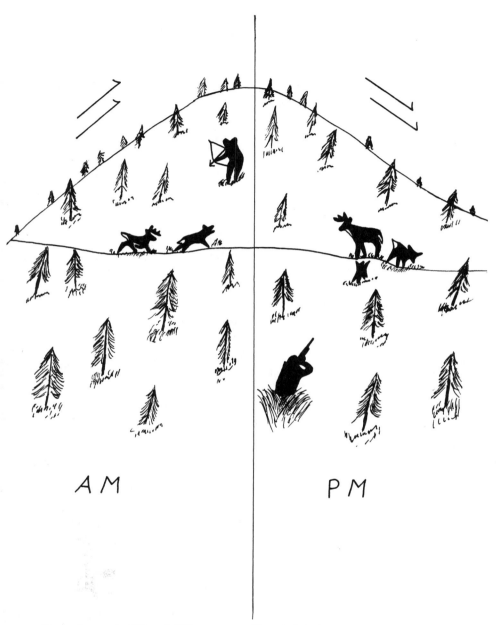

AM

PM

Thermal currents. If there is little or no prevailing wind, the hunter should position himself above the deer trail in the morning and below the trail in the latter part of the afternoon.

evening the flow is reversed—air comes down along the side of the hill. Be above the trail in the morning and below it at sunset—if there are no prevailing winds which indicate otherwise. Because of the wind it is always advisable to have at least two stands.

In heavily-hunted areas your best chance of success is at a stand along an escape route. These trails head to and through the heaviest brush. You find escape routes in the lowlands and cedar and pine groves, and leading into and out of swamps. Without fail, the best escape routes connect two pieces of ground to enable deer to complete a circle.

TYPES OF STANDS

First let me describe the *ground stand*. You must make this carefully, especially if you use short-range equipment such as bow and arrow. Building a ground stand is not difficult but it does take a lot of planning. When deciding where to construct the stand, wind direction is the most vital consideration. Because you cannot move a stand from place to place, you must determine which way the winds usually blow and if thermal currents will affect you. Build accordingly.

The stand should be near enough to cover to allow deer to approach and pass you by. It must break up your visual image, or completely conceal you from view. This is very important if you intend to call bucks or rattle antlers. If the animal feels that he can come to the source of the call unseen he will be less hesitant and you will get a closer shot.

The stand should be made weeks before the season so the deer get used to its presence. The stand should be made of natural materials from the immediate vicinity. Ground stands made of cedar or pine branches are best because these trees keep their foliage longer unless disturbed. A stand made from broadleaf branches—such as oak or maple—causes some small problems. In 4–5 days the branches will become dry—and noisy when touched. Their leaves drop easily so you must constantly rebuild and add on to your stand.

Commercial camouflage nets or cloths are great—provided they don't have a shine to them—because they completely hide your body and legs. You can add camouflage to the outside of a cloth or net to make it much more realistic.

Whatever material is used for a ground stand, a tree should be part of it. This helps break up the image of both you and your stand.

The stand's size is also very important. It must allow the hunter and his equipment freedom to maneuver in all directions he expects to shoot. Archers need plenty of room above their heads and in fromt of them so their bow won't hit or get tangled in the stand. The sides should be as high as the hunter's head while he is in his waiting position.

Being on the ground means you cannot fidget or move around very much, so you must make yourself as comfortable as possible. A seat is a must. Find a log or old stump or dig a small hole and make a ledge to sit on. The floor must be free of leaves, for if they get dry they get very noisy and announce your presence well in advance.

On the ground, you're at your quarry's eye level. Deer pick up the glare and reflection from your skin immediately, so camouflage makeup must include the hands and face.

All movement on the ground must be extremely slow and deliberate. Search with your eyes and ears instead of your head and neck— this will pay off in venison steaks and chops.

The tree stand. If allowed by law, this is by far the best way to stack the odds in your favor if you have a short-range weapon. Above ground level, your scent is carried off over the deer's head. This doesn't in any way mean that you should not wear cover-up scent however. Damp, wet air will carry your diluted scent down to the deer as will a thermal draft.

Slow movement isn't readily noticed in a tree stand because deer don't usually look for danger from above. However, because of their excellent peripheral vision they often spot the slightest movement by hunters less than 10 feet above the ground. Not taking that point into consideration has cost me several deer in past years.

For the archer, I don't recommend going higher than 15 feet above the ground because the higher you go, the smaller the vital target area. Also, you have to shoot down at the deer, so the arrow must penetrate the deer's bony and meatier back. Another reason for not going high is the difficulty of shooting down at a steep angle accurately.

Bowhunters in trees make two mistakes. They forget to bend at the waist (this puts pressure on the bottom of the bow grip and causes the arrow to shoot high). And they misjudge distance. Many think the

A permanent tree stand with roof and sides to protect the hunter from the elements and conceal him from the deer.

deer is farther away than he really is. They should estimate the distance from the base of the tree to the deer, not from the bow to the deer. These two errors often produce misses and bad hits. As sportsmen and conservationists we do not want either.

Another reason tree stands are good is that you can cover a 360-degree field of fire. Visibility is excellent. You can see more clearly and farther, and this gives you time to get ready in advance.

Safety is another benefit: a man in a tree stand is above other hunters' line of fire.

Comfort is yet another reason to select a tree stand: it can be made as comfortable as you want. Some have sides to break the wind, a roof to shed rain—even a heater to keep the hunter warm as he sits on a cushion!

A permanent tree stand, if allowed in your area, should be built well before the season so deer will get used to its presence and forget about all the racket you made building it.

Permanent stands should be roomy enough to move around in and should be free of limb obstructions. They should have side panels to at least cover your legs in case a deer looks up at the new structure in his domain. The most important consideration—besides the location—is to pick a stout tree. When a cold wind blows you don't want the tree to sway or the stand to creak. If you can, put carpet or burlap on the floor to muffle your boots.

One of the greatest innovations in deer hunting is the portable tree stand. With it, the hunter is free to move about from one location to another at will. Choose a portable tree stand that you feel comfortable in and one that will fit your hunting style. Some are more comfortable than others but are much too bulky to quietly reassemble should you decide to move during the day. If you are going to stay in your stand more than four hours at a time, get one that allows you to sit down. If you like to move from spot to spot or stillhunt part of the day, get a stand you can strap to your back.

Commercial portable stands are usually better than homemade ones—at least the one I tried to make once.

Quite a while back, when I was new to bowhunting, I was using a permanent tree stand that was great for shotguns and rifles but not acceptable for bow and arrow because all the good trails were just out of range. At that time I could not afford a portable stand and it was too late to build a stand near the run I wanted to hunt.

Portable tree stands offer mobility, which is a necessity, as wind and seasonal change determine which trails deer will most often use. As you can see, the investment is worth it.

So one morning I borrowed my father's stepladder and a long, heavy strap for a safety belt. Before sunrise I set the ladder up against a big tree on the side of a hill near the trail, climbed up, and strapped myself to the tree. I had just squared away when a buck appeared at the top of the hill and proceeded straight toward me. Unfortunately I was not in position. I had to turn around slowly to come to full draw. I felt the ladder move a bit as I took aim at the six-pointer just 15 yards away.

As I released the arrow, the ladder shot out from under me. I missed the buck and was left dangling from the tree a few inches above the ground. After I cut myself loose I went out and bought a safe, portable stand. I can laugh about it now but it scared the hell out of me then.

As a last resort, you can use the crotch of a tree. I have taken many deer from this uncomfortable position—several just recently. When using a limb or crotch of a tree, get as comfortable as possible and clear away any limbs that may catch your bow or interfere with your shooting.

Whatever kind of stand you try, estimate the distance to all the trails or possible target areas as soon as you set up. If you have a rangefinder as part of your equipment, now is the time to use it. Don't wait until the deer arrive, because you may not have enough time.

16

Hunting the Heavily Hunted Areas

Using competing hunters to your advantage is important today. To do this well, you must not only understand the whitetail's reaction to men in the woods, but also the habits of most modern-day hunters. Most hunters venture into the woods around sunrise and leave around 10 a.m., partly because they believe the deer have bedded down for the day by that time and partly because they have become tired, restless, or cold. Some leave at that time to put on a drive which lasts 'til around noon, and those that haven't left by then will do so by noon . . .

All, that is, except those of us who take advantage of the deer movement caused by the traveling hunters. We wait until 12:30 and set up again before 1 p.m. to take advantage of the movement caused by the drives and returning stand hunters and stalkers.

Deer drives will continue, in most areas, until about two hours before dusk. At that time, most hunters take their evening stands. By doing so they continue to move the deer around the woods. If you have been standing in an escape area, you will probably see quite a few deer every day.

That brings us to the most important step: picking the right spot to stand. I have already described the type of cover needed for an escape route. Some places along those routes are better than others when hunters are present.

For instance, I have noticed while hunting on a hill or small mountain that the best stands are at or near the top. Elusive deer cross the top constantly when being pushed from one hideout to another—that is why I recommend those locations for two-man drives. When making their escape, deer usually come up from the base of the hill by way of the steepest grade they can manage, provided it offers good cover. Once on top they stop to check behind them. If there is a small plateau or ledge in this area, they will go to it and stay there awhile to keep an eye on things. If none is available, they will probably continue to seek cover or remain at the base of the hill and continue to circle. The best areas are saplings, or cedar, or pine stands, but any very heavy brush is good.

Hunting on flat land can be a challenge unless you know the area or have a map of it. In this terrain, deer elude hunters numerous ways and will not stick to any set pattern. However, instinct directs them to certain areas, and when hunting pressure becomes tense, the slick little critters follow their instincts.

The best areas are those that seem almost impenetrable to hunters. They usually contain high standing and thick brush connecting two sections of heavy terrain. These areas can be readily identified as escape routes by the narrow trails leading into the brush and a tunnel-like trail in the middle. If you wish to enter the brush, you have to get down on your hands and knees and crawl inside to the tunnel. Should you decide to go inside, I strongly advise that you wear plenty of bright-colored clothing to protect you from itchy fingers and vivid imaginations. On more than one occasion hunters have sworn I had long ears and antlers.

I was brought up hunting on farmland, so, to me, it is the easiest of all areas to score in. The land is not only conveniently broken up into patches of different shapes and sizes, but there are low brush lines around the fields and enough food to keep the deer well fed and hidden. Because deer are browsers, you can depend on them to expose themselves at least once a day in a crop field. Usually they come out about two hours before sunset if hunting pressure is light. When it is heavy, they will generally wait until dark before venturing into the open to browse.

If competition is stiff, let the other hunters wait at the field edges. Walk deeper into the woods where they are narrow or peninsula-shaped. Deer hang out in these areas for some time before venturing forth to face so many intruders.

The key is to know where the other hunters are and then to be somewhere else, because that's where the deer will be.

Let them chase the deer to you.

17

Maps

If you or your friends are unfamiliar with an area, then you should use a map. In fact, it is not a bad idea to have one with you even if you *are* familiar with the area. A map gives you a better idea of what you are doing or what you *should* be doing. You can plan exactly where to place standers and drivers, which way to progress from one drive to another, and which type of drive to use. A map can answer almost any question you have and suggest others you have not yet asked.

By marking your moves on the map you can tell why or how deer gave you the slip, and when you score, your map serves as a reference point for future drives.

A topographic or "topo" map tells you the name of an area's principal landmarks and the section of the state where they are located. It has a scale on miles and/or feet for plotting distance. The map shows magnetic declination so you can correct your compass, shows both magnetic and geographic north, and gives the code numbers for maps that match your map, should you decide to hunt a larger area.

The topo map shows actual terrain. Such features as forests, rivers, swamps, water holes, streams, and peaks are indicated by symbols. Contour lines help you determine slope—this is the most valuable feature.

Topo maps also indicate roads, buildings, towns, and jeep and pack and hiking trails.

For future reference, mark the best habitat on the map as you walk.

With this abundance of detailed information you can plan drives and stalks effectively. You can tell where the best hunting is.

The only hitch is that United States Geological Survey Maps may be ten or more years old. Some current roads or buildings may not be marked on the map, and some trails and fire roads may be overgrown. Some streams and lakes may be dry from time to time, so carry extra water.

To secure a U.S.G.S. map for areas east of the Mississippi River, write to:

> Washington Map Distribution Center
> United States Geological Survey
> 1200 Eads Ave.
> Arlington, VA 22202

For areas west of the Mississippi River write to:

> United States Geological Survey
> Federal Center, Bldg. 41
> Denver, Colorado 80225

For Canada write to:

> Canada Map Office
> 615 Booth St.
> Ottawa, Ontario
> Canada K1A OE9

Forest Service maps.   A hunter can also use a Forest Service map although it doesn't have contour lines. This map shows access roads and other man-made structures so you can get a general idea of where you are. In the flatlands they are quite acceptable.

To obtain Forest Service maps write to:

U.S. Dept. of Agriculture
Forest Services
Washington, D.C. 20250

Ask for brochure No. FS-13, Field Offices of the Forest Service. This brochure lists the ten regional offices from which the Forest Service maps may be obtained.

18

Deer and Dogs—and Wolves

Where did all the deer go? There were several of them here just before the season. You will find part of the answer in this section.

In much of the south it is legal to use dogs for hunting deer. The habitat in these areas is mostly thick underbrush and swamp. In such areas as Florida, hunters who use dogs make up two-thirds of all successful hunters.

What is of special interest is the deer's response to dogs. A study done in Georgia using radio-monitored whitetail deer noted some interesting characteristics of deer's ability to elude dogs. Their evasive tactics patterns resemble those they use when pressured by many hunters.

The deers' maneuvers were classified into five categories of escape pattern: holding, distance running, circuitous (zig-zag) running, separating from a group, and using escape habitat.

Holding.   If the cover is heavy deer will allow dogs to come as close as a few yards before breaking into a run. This tactic often results in the dogs passing the deer and following a different trail. As I mentioned earlier, deer often do this when men walk through the woods. In the Georgia tests, this maneuver worked four out of seven times.

Distance running. In this maneuver deer ran relatively straight courses for a long distance, quickly leaving their home range, and using speed and endurance to lose the hounds. This maneuver always worked. In seven occurrences, three deer lost the dogs every time. It should be noted that the investigators found that adult bucks tend to run in a straight course and quickly leave the home range area.

Circuitous (zig-zag) running. Here deer ran a complicated, circular, zig-zag pattern, frequently crossing their own trails while never leaving their home range. This pattern often caused the dogs to switch to the trail of a different deer. If the hounds managed to stay on the original trail they eventually dropped too far behind to follow the scent. The dogs were usually unable to chase the deer rapidly even though the deer made brief stops at frequent intervals during the chase, probably to check their trails. When the hounds closed in again, the chase resumed. This pattern was exhibited by all deer studied and the dogs lost the trails in 10 of 19 instances.

Separating. The deer tagged with instruments separated themselves from other deer. This resulted in the dogs pursuing other members of the group. In some cases, the tagged deer separated from the group at the initiation of the chase; in others, they remained with the group for part of the chase. Occasionally the tagged deer came into temporary contact with other deer while being pursued. Separating from the group was exhibited by 5 deer and the dogs were eluded in 13 of 17 instances.

The study also found that deer in areas with high populations were more difficult to chase for extended periods than those in low populations.

Using habitat. Deer ran through water, making it difficult for the dogs to follow the trail. This was recorded in 40 cases and caused the dogs to lose the trail in all but two cases. Research found that 42 percent of the deer escaped the hounds without the aid of water, so, although the deer apparently did not require water for escape, they readily used swamps or other bodies of water when available.

One of the most significant findings, I believe, is that in 78 percent of the cases the deer left their home ranges when pursued. Most of them remained within one mile of their home range, however, and some returned during the chase. With one exception, all deer returned to their home ranges within one day. While returning, they usually moved at a fast walk or trot and took the most direct routes to their ranges rather than back-tracking along the chase routes. This means that when hunters invade the woods on opening day you might not see deer in an area that had plenty just a day earlier. If deer leave an area because of dogs they will do the same because of hunters. From this information it is apparent that slow-running hounds benefit the hunter. The slower pace allows the deer to stop frequently to check their trails and to run at a slower pace. This in turn allows the hunter to make a well-placed shot.

HUNTING NEAR WOLF PACKS

Wildlife research has uncovered some information which could be very useful to sportsmen wishing to hunt areas where there are wolf pack territories.

The studies of the deer-wolf interactions were prompted by a severe decline in whitetail populations in the remote Boundary Waters Canoe Area (BWCA), in the Superior National Forest of northeastern Minnesota.

In that area deer had succumbed to wolf predation, a series of hard winters, and maturing vegetation.

To help unveil some new information as well as support older theories on deer-wolf interactions, researchers livetrapped, ran health checks, radio collared, and released both deer and wolves.

One of their findings was that all of the deer had at least one major waterway, beaver pond, or small lake bordering their summer ranges to use as a means of escape from the wolves.

Also found was that densities of whitetail populations are higher in areas of wolf "buffer zones" (territory overlaps) than in territory centers. Although research is still seeking new information about the pack's use of its buffer zone, there are some important known facts. There is a peripheral strip perhaps two kilometers wide which borders each territory. This strip—buffer zone—is scent marked (mostly in winter) and traveled on by packs on either side of the strip. Because of possible encounters with neighboring packs, this is an area of insecurity, so neither pack spends much time there. The size of the strip allows for the possible support of a considerable amount of deer.

Except when food becomes scarce, the buffer zones between territories remain in about the same locations over the years. This boundary stability not only maintains peace between packs, it also helps maintain reservoirs of deer that may disperse into cores of pack territories. This is of great importance when deer numbers decline. When this happens wolf numbers also decline, so deer from buffer zones could then increase and repopulate territory cores.

It is evident that wolves seldom kill deer along territory edges unless desperate.

Researchers have also found that deer in wolf areas will not only have higher concentrations in buffer zones but also near human populations. There, fewer wolves are present, thus adding safety to the deer. The researchers have also noted the average minimum life span of a deer living in a buffer zone to be a minimum of 8 years. This may also indicate that, if the habitat is good, there may be a record-sized buck in such areas.

What all this information may suggest to a hunter or wildlife observer is that once you have located the buffer zone (ask the local conservation official), you have also located an area that will offer a high probability of success.

19

Winter Hunting

Late season hunting is being offered to more and more sportsmen. My home state has a January bow season, and for those of us willing to venture out into the January winds, it is a welcome event.

Before the hunter decides to stand out in inhospitable weather, he should become aware of some of the changes nature has wrought. In the northern half of the country there is snow and cutting wind this time of year. To humans, snow is beautiful and a lot of fun; to deer, it is more threatening than beneficial.

If snow should reach ¾ of the way to a deer's chest he is severely hampered and must jump from spot to spot. This not only takes a lot of energy, it makes him easy prey for dogs and wolves. Snow also covers the already-dwindling food supply, causing deer to burn more precious calories locating buried food. Fortunately, nature lowers deer's metabolism to help compensate for the lack of food.

With their metabolism lowered, deer do not eat as much—even if there is an abundance of food. However, in nature abundance is seldom found. The buck, having lost about 25 percent of his weight during the rut, comes into the winter in poorer condition than the doe.

He and the growing fawn have the toughest time surviving the winter if there is a lot of snow.

Winter also changes the feeding and movement patterns of deer. They now feed during the day and bed during the night, because it is easier to locate food during daylight and the air gets warmer, which saves precious calories. Even if they don't migrate, deer congregate and move from their normal habitat to the shelter of draws, gulleys, and thick evergreen swamps. This winter grouping area is called the deer yard.

In the deer yard they are protected from wind and the snow is not as deep. The thick, dark growth attracts and holds the heat of the day well into the night.

Unfortunately, food is often scarce because the deer have a habit of returning to the same yarding area year after year, giving the deer yard little chance to recover from the previous year's heavy browsing.

However, it is not food which draws deer to the yard, but the security. Without fail, shelter has priority over food. This preference for security, as illogical as it may appear to us, has enabled deer to survive millions of years.

When the weather breaks, they venture forth to find food. Usually you find them on the south, west, and southeast slopes of steep mountains or ridges. Here the vegetation is usually heaviest and the snow not so deep. Because the south side is warm, they bed there whenever possible. They seek whatever browse they can find: red maple sprouts, white cedar, and yew are some favorites, as are new shoots which grow from tree stumps. If the food supply is low, deer sometimes eat such ''stuffer'' forage as red cedar, balsam, or rhododendron. When they start feeding heavily on stuffer foods, they are in danger of losing the fight for survival.

SNOW HUNTING

A white camouflage outfit with black patches is ideal for snow hunting because it breaks up a full white image and is thus more natural-looking in a wooded area. Most people hunting in cold weather spend as little time as possible in the field. If deer are yarded and you know where the yard is, you can make your stay in the field short, even if you have a short-range weapon.

Deep or crunchy snow makes a silent approach nearly impossible.

With so many eyes searching for danger, you are likely to be spotted if you try to get too close. You must encourage deer to leave their security and burn off some previous energy.

I have found the best way to do this is to cover your scent with a fox lure and walk upwind within 100 yards of the yard. Spray a tree or bush with the scent of one of their favorite foods native to the area. (If they are not familiar with the scent they may not respond. However, occasionally I have found that deer leave their beds to check out a new scent, possibly in hopes of trying out a strange food.) After the scent has been applied, quietly and quickly take a stand 20 yards crosswind of the scent and wait. If they haven't been spooked, and the snow is not too deep, at least a few deer will approach cautiously to investigate.

I would like to mention something about winter equipment for the bow-hunter. Be sure that your bow has a quiet arrow rest and a lightly-cushioned sight window or arrowplate. When the first winter season opened here, I was shaking so badly from the cold I had trouble holding the arrow still as I nocked it. It rattled against the bow and spooked a fine buck who still had half his antlers.

20

Habitat and Increasing Deer Populations

The need for improved habitat becomes obvious, especially when one inspects a deer yard. It is here that the elements take their toll most heavily. Here the condition of the habitat can be best observed.

Probably the best indication of the food supply in a given yard is the browse line, which shows how far the deer must reach up—balancing precariously on their hind legs—to get food. The browse line is usually most noticeable on stuffer forage. If the browse line reaches as high as seven feet—the height a mature buck can usually reach—starvation threatens. This is so because yearlings may only be able to reach as high as five feet, and does about six. Fawns are in critical danger at this point.

Another indication of a critical food shortage is the size of the twigs the deer feed on. When food is plentiful, deer eat younger shoots because they have more bark. (It is the bark of young twigs that contains the nutrients, not the hard-to-digest bark and cellulose of older and woodier twigs.) As food becomes less available, deer are forced to seek the less nutritious twigs up to ¼ inch in diameter. In extreme cold, eating thick, frozen twigs burns up as much energy as it produces because wood fiber must be warmed by body heat as it is digested.

A browse line is evident on these cedars. This indicates a lack of food for the population of deer in this area. A browse line destroys the habitat for many years to come. *Photo by Leonard Lee Rue III.*

You can also tell by looking at deer how well they are holding up against the elements. A deer in good shape is a beautiful creature of sleek, rounded lines. His back will be nearly flat with a small graceful curve at the shoulder and an almost-unnoticeable curve at the rump. His neck is full and rounded.

As his small fat reserves diminish, his shoulders show a pronounced hump and his hips acquire a downward slant. (A hunter who has skinned a thriving deer knows that there is quite a bit of fat at the rump area.) His ribs start to show and his neck seems longer because it is thinner.

As starvation nears, a deer stands with his back humped, and to increase resistance to cold, he makes his hair stand on end. If he has

As food gets scarce, deer must reach high. Deer that cannot reach high enough will soon be in big trouble. *Photo by Leonard Lee Rue III.*

Note starving doe's protruding shoulder and rump lines and thin neck. *Photo by Leonard Lee Rue III.*

Note the humped back and puffed fur of this fawn trying to keep his body heat. At this point he is very close to death. *Photo by Leonard Lee Rue III.*

lost more than 30 percent of his body weight, it is doubtful he will survive, even with the aid of food.

It has been observed that deer don't leave the security of their deer yard to reach food even as nearby as 100 yards away. They remain at the yard until the snow melts enough to permit easy travel. For a fawn, that may mean less than 12 inches of snow. By the time snow cover shrinks to that point, it may be too late for many. We can't change this instinct to "yard," but we can increase the food supply in known yarding areas and nearby. Feeding deer by hand has been proven a temporary benefit at best, and in areas where there are dogs— domestic or wild—or other predators, it is unfavorable. The packing of the snow by snowmobiles and men's feet makes it easy for predators to chase the yarded deer. They have little chance to escape and if they do they use up much-needed and often irreplaceable energy.

Aerial feeding is better, but this is expensive and, again, the results are at best temporary.

Modern machinery leaves little if anything for wildlife to live on during the winter months.

Power right-of-ways, though unsightly, offer good browse for deer and cover for smaller creatures.

Educating the public to the value of game management and the increasing of habitat and its quality can help prevent such scenes as this in the years to come.

A better method is burning and/or cutting. This causes new growth, and new growth means high quality browse. The better the browse, the more deer.

This is not to say that without increased winter food the species is doomed. Survival instincts have kept deer around for millions of years without the aid of man. The question is, do we want this species— and wildlife in general—to continue to increase in numbers and remain healthy? ''Positively!'' is the only answer to that question.

Increasing habitat, or at least improving existing habitat, has benefits other than getting deer through the winter. Quality habitat also helps determine reproduction and the number of bucks born.

Research has found that when habitat is good and the area not over-crowded, yearling does are highly receptive to breeding. It has also been determined that yearling does produce more bucks than older does. Also, better habitat makes heavier bucks with bigger racks.

At present, many states are successfully experimenting with chemicals and fertilizer to improve habitat. These experiments are expensive, and thus restricted. Perhaps these tests will prove fertilization economical and it will be put to use on a large scale. In the meantime, we should encourage conservation departments to increase burn and cut and to plant better browse in critical areas. It would also be an improvement to expand the nation's parks system. It benefits all of us for generations to come.

21

The Shot

There are times—and I wish there were more such times—when while hunting or taking photographs you are confronted with two or more spectacular bucks. You don't have much time to decide which one to take. You want the best one. How do you choose?

Fortunately, there is a reliable measure of antlered animals. For the whitetail, blacktail, mule deer, and pronghorn antelope, it is the ears.

A whitetail's ears are about 6 inches long from the white spot at the base to the tip. I use the white spot because it is easy to see at a distance. The spread from ear tip to ear tip is about 14 inches as the ears rest alongside and in front of the antlers.

To qualify for the record books, deer need an inside antler spread at least a few inches wider than the spread of their ear tips. The main beam should be at least four times the length of the ears. The long tines should be uniform and at least five on a side. And, of course, the heavier the rack, the better the score.

If you are fortunate enough to have such a buck in front of you, I hope you have practiced well and don't come up with a sudden case of buck fever.

BUCK FEVER

I had just made myself comfortable under a low-hanging pine branch when I heard a branch snap behind me. The buck walked steadily through heavy brush and was headed toward the safety of a nearby swamp. As he reached a clearing just 20 yards away I could see that he had eight points. My heart was pounding so loudly I thought for sure the buck would hear it.

I raised my slightly-shaking shotgun and pointed it at his lungs. I fired. The buck went down but kept kicking.

Then he started to drag himself away with his front legs. Excited, I quickly fired two more rounds at him. He kept going. Quickly, I reloaded and ran up to him. At point blank range, I put one round through his neck and ended the struggle.

Shaking now more than ever, I tried to figure out how he had kept moving with three loads of buckshot in him.

You have only a few seconds to decide. Which one would you choose? *Photo by Leonard Lee Rue III.*

Later, when we skinned him, I found out why: "buck fever."
Only one pellet from the first round had hit him. Fortunately, it had
hit his spine and paralyzed his hind legs. The other two rounds missed
him—at just 20 yards!

Bewildered, I began to think back. Sure enough, when I was
pointing the shotgun at him, I was *looking at the deer and not down
the barrel*. My cheek was not against the stock of the gun. This caused
the barrel to be aimed high, causing a near miss. The other two shots
were worse because I was overexcited. I was only 14 then, but that
near miss has taught me a lesson I will never forget.

Just how many times a year this happens we will never know.
However, there is a cure for hunters who can't seem to bring down
deer they have (or thought they have) hit.

The first step is to admit that they have buck fever. It is nothing
to be ashamed of. We all get excited before making a shot. A man
who refuses to admit that he gets a bit too excited will never muster
up the necessary self-control to hit a target consistently.

The second part of the cure is to stop and think before you shoot.
This is best done by taking at least one deep breath before bringing
up the gun or bow and taking aim. This momentary rest calms your
nerves and reduces shaking. With steady hands, you are sure to score.

Third, prescout your hunting area. Get to know it and some of
the deer in it. Familiarity breeds confidence and confidence lessens
nervousness.

SHOT PROFILES

Sometimes the direction and speed a deer travels—and the habitat—limit the target area and timing of the shot. Even with these
complications, there is usually always a vital area exposed. However,
there are shots that give clean, fast kills and which all sportsmen should
look for.

Broadside shots.   A broadside shot is always the best for a quick,
clean kill. There is less muscle and there are fewer non-vital organs
to hamper deep penetration. There is less chance of bone deflection,
and the broadside angle offers a larger target and better view of the
vital areas than any other profile.

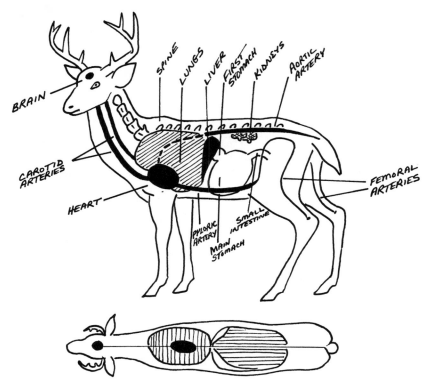

Frontal shots. The frontal view is narrow and neck muscles present a penetration problem so a clean kill is less likely. Here, one should aim low and on the center line of the neck and chest. If you hit here, you have a good chance to break the neck and/or pierce the lungs or heart.

Because of the narrow target, there is a higher chance of a nonlethal wound—especially with an arrow. Another drawback is that you may be spotted because the deer will probably be looking in your direction. Slow, careful movement is of the utmost importance in this instance.

Quartering shot. The quartering-away shot is another good shot. Although it offers less of a view of the organs, the hunter is out of the deer's field of view and can move to steady himself for an accurate shot. Penetration is not hampered by bone and the bullet or arrow goes deep into the vital chest cavity for a fast clean kill.

Rump shot.   A shot at the rump or going-away profile is by far the poorest choice and is not recommended. This shot must be made at the back of the neck or directly between the legs. A fast, slow-opening bullet is best used here, but as I pointed out in the cartridge section, you will probably not carry this type of bullet. The archer gets deeper penetration than the rifle hunter but even then this shot is near impossible for most bowhunters. Very little if any blood for tracking is produced because the deer usually bleeds internally. Although the femoral arteries are near the target area, you need luck to hit either— and if not completely severed they do not make much of a blood trail for very long, so you will probably lose the deer. At this angle, the spine is hard to hit for even the most experienced hunter, especially if the deer is walking or running.

At this angle a shotgun presents your best chance because there is a possibility the spreading pellets will hit the legs and put the deer down for a second shot.

Head shot.   A shot at the head will put the deer down immediately. However, few hunters are able to keep their sights on this small and highly mobile target. Unless the brain is struck, the deer will soon recover and will leave very little if any blood to trail. If you find that you must shoot at this target, wait until he has his head down. It is likely to remain stationary longer while in this position.

DEER REACTIONS WHEN SHOT

The question always arises about how far a deer travels when hit and how he reacts when hit. Obviously these questions are very complex, but from my own experience and observations made while tracking numerous deer for myself and other hunters over the years, I have come to the following conclusions.

How a wounded deer reacts depends on numerous variables: arrow weight, penetration, and sharpness (bow); bullet shape, speed, and shocking power (firearm); and vital organs injured in both cases.

Another factor is whether or not the deer was standing calmly or had been running before the shot (which increases the adrenaline in his system).

Brain, spine, and neck.   Vertebrae shots drop a deer immediately. (He may not die immediately though.) Anyone making a spinal shot should immediately shoot again at the heart or lungs. These shots are the most difficult for an inexperienced hunter to make.

Archers should avoid all these targets because they are easily missed and the arrow may not sever the spinal cord. The result will be a superficial wound. The two deer I have taken with brain shots were five to seven yards away—and I took the shots only because I had been spotted.

Lungs.   The lungs are the best spot to shoot at. The target area is large and the kill, although seldom instantaneous, usually takes less than 10 seconds if both lungs are hit. A deer hit here may hunch up and kick out with his hind legs before making a hard run in a straight line. About 30 yards later he begins to slow down and perhaps succumb to the injury. A deer seldom travels more than 80 yards with such a wound.

A hit in only one lung can mean long tracking—600 yards or more. An archer needs to get deep penetration and a rifleman must use a softpoint bullet with a thin jacket. The wound will yield pinkish, frothy blood. Picking up the trail will be easy, as the deer will leave a trail almost instantly. Blood may spray on the vegetation as much as five feet from his tracks.

A hit in the lower part of the lung produces a better blood trail than a hit in the upper part. Even if you are not sure if both lungs were hit you can begin tracking within five minutes of the shot.

Heart.   A deer responds to this hit like a lung hit except that he may jump wildly the instant he is hit—almost as though a shock had passed through his body. The blood is dark red and he leaves only a thin or spotty trail. The lack of blood shouldn't worry you though, because deer hit this way usually can travel only about 30 yards—never as far as 80 yards—before coming to rest. You can track in just 5 or 10 minutes. If you can't find the blood trail, simply walk in a circle (the technique is described more fully later). You will find it.

Liver.   When hit in the liver, a deer may hunch up and take a few quick steps or leap, with his tail tucked under him, then slowly walk away. I saw one buck walk 10 yards, then stand beside a tree for over a minute before he succumbed to the wound. Had my arrow hit the renal artery in the liver, death would have been nearly instantaneous. Most liver shots restrict the deer's travel to less than 80 yards and kill him in less than 5 minutes. I say "usually" because a partial or shallow hit in the liver may allow a deer to travel several hundred yards.

On suspected liver shots, you should wait 20 minutes before tracking. When tracking a deer with a liver wound, proceed as quietly and slowly as possible. If you don't find him within 80–100 yards, take a break for about 20 minutes or so, then continue tracking. If you are running out of daylight, take it slow and mark your trail well and track until dark.

Kidney.   This shot, although not very common, causes a relatively fast kill of about 5 minutes. Deer react to kidney shots as to liver shots, but often walk a bit faster for 30 yards or so before slowing down. After a 10- or 15-minute wait, follow the thin trail of dark blood. Deer hit this way seldom travel more than 90 yards.

Arteries.   Not all quick kills come from hits in the vital organs. Some are caused by hits in the major arteries. Although these hits are made by accident, they are nevertheless fatal and should be studied because they cause tracking problems.

The information that follows refers to complete severing of the arteries in question.

As a general rule, when an artery is hit a deer clamps his tail down and runs several yards, then checks his trail before continuing.

Aorta. The number one artery in the body is the aorta. This artery delivers blood to most of the body and runs from the heart up to and along the spine. Severing this artery drops a deer within 40 yards, so you will probably see him go down. After 20 minutes go and get him. If you don't see or hear him go down, the blood trail will be wide and very easy to follow.

Renal artery. The renal artery also produces a quick kill, and as indicated in the kidney section, the deer will not travel far or fast. The blood trail is not as obvious as the aorta's but it should be constant.

Carotid arteries. These run up the neck just under the windpipe. Deer hit here leave a wide trail of pink blood—as in a lung hit. Deer seldom travel more than 120 yards unless pushed, so it would be wise to wait at least 20 minutes before tracking.

Pyloric artery. This serves the stomach and intestinal area. A hit here causes a bright red trail. A deer can travel 150 yards with a hit here, so the waiting time should be no less than a half hour. Track this wound very slowly.

Femoral arteries. A hit here can cause problems. If you don't completely sever the artery, you will have to do quite a bit of tracking. Under ideal conditions, bright red blood starts a good trail within yards of where the deer was hit. A bright red blood trail is thin but easily read, and deer normally travel less than 125 yards before dying. I don't believe it is necessary to wait longer than 10 minutes before starting to track.

Once I have determined that a femoral artery has been only partly severed, I give the deer a half-hour head start then begin tracking him slowly. Whenever the blood begins to thin, I wait about 10 minutes then start again. This gives the deer a chance to stop and leave a few spurts of blood for me to find.

If after 200 yards or so, I find the blood trail nearly gone, with watery pinhead drops, I figure he is either healing (deer blood clots easily) or is ready to or has dropped. If he is healing, you will lose him if you don't make him open the wound by moving. You have little choice but to put pressure on him.

If I find no blood trail, I mark the last spot and push on in the direction he was taking. This makes him move—if he is conscious—and give his presence away. I can then close in to finish him off.

GUT SHOTS

Still another problem is the gut or paunch shot. This area includes the stomach and intestines and small veins and arteries near them.

A paunch-shot deer hunches up and clamps his tail down. The blood is dark red—almost like that from a flesh wound—and if from the stomach, a green or brown tint will be evident. The blood trail is spotty and there will be times when no blood is found at all because the wound bled internally.

A paunch-shot deer seldom dies sooner than 15 or 16 hours after being hit, or travels more than 150 yards, so you would be wise to leave the area as quietly as possible and come back later. Be sure to mark the area and remember which trail and direction the deer took. When you return, track slowly and be ready to make a fast shot should he still be alive.

HAIR

Sometimes rain washes away blood trails and tracks.

Hair left at the scene may indicate the area of the hit, and you can estimate how far the deer may travel before going down.

Having a hunting partner or two is a great help, because you each can circle in various directions to pick up a trail or sign.

Depending on the time of the year, the hair density and length varies. In summer the coat is short and thick and has solid hair. Closer to winter, the hair becomes long and hollow. The tips become darker.

All this must be considered in the analysis.

The example discussed below is a 125-pound (dressed) buck harvested just before the rut. The deer is of the *O.v. borealis* species.

Lungs.   Hair in the lung area is dark brown and in some cases almost blue-gray. It is thick and about 1¼–1½ inches long just behind the shoulder. Hair over the front shoulder is 1–1¼ inches long, lighter in color, and thicker.

Heart.   Heart area hair is about 2¼–2½ inches long and lighter in color than lung area hair. A frontal shot to the heart leaves hair that is light-colored (gray or white-tipped) and about one inch long; one to the exact center of the brisket leaves a tuft brown to dark gray in color.

Neck.   Hair over the neck is also only about one inch long and lighter in color than that of the lung area. Just under the jawbone the hair is white and dense but short.

Stomach.   Hair along the stomach bottom is white or gray, about 3 inches long and coarse.

Back and hindquarters.   Along the spinal column, in the middle

Hair length and color can indicate just where you hit your deer.

section, the hair is a little darker and longer than that of the lung area. Here the hair is about 1¾ to two inches long. The hair closer to the neck and rump is heavier, shorter and lighter in color.

The hair on the hindquarters is about one inch long, dense, and like that of the front leg area: light in color.

Tail. The tail is brown on the top side and the hair length on the bottom is over three inches long and white.

AFTER THE SHOT

If the deer is moving slowly or browsing before the shot, the hunter should not make any noise immediately after shooting unless the deer bolts more than 20 yards away. There are a few reasons for this. If you make a clean miss, the deer may not know where the noise came from and may remain where he is. This is especially true in bowhunting. Often, though, a deer will jump or run a few steps then stop to check the area. This may give you another shot at a standing deer. The exception here is when hunting with a shotgun with buck shot: the loud report coupled with the noise of pellets hitting surrounding brush and trees sends the deer off on a fast circular run.

Another reason for remaining silent is that if you score a good hit, the deer isn't likely to panic and will take cover much sooner, making tracking much easier. Also, deer that don't run after being shot tend to yield better-tasting meat.

Still another reason is that deer seldom travel alone. Even during the rut, subordinate bucks will travel with the large bucks. If you down one, the others often come back within 15 minutes to check on their companion. If the deer call out with a grunting sound, they will return shortly. If you are hunting with a friend, he may cash in—I have done so a number of times over the years.

22

Tracking Wounded Game

The most important part of hunting is to locate the game that you shoot. It is not hard to master this skill, yet many hunters fail to. Perhaps they think they are such good shots that the game is just going to fall over dead when they shoot. Or maybe they haven't been told how to go about it. For the sake of hunting's future I hope this pattern soon changes.

The first step is to locate where the deer was standing when hit. For archers it helps to know exactly where the arrow struck the deer.

The next step is to estimate the distance the deer had traveled when last seen. At long ranges make a mental note of nearby natural objects such as trees or bushes.

Next, mark the spot from which you shot with a white or brightly-colored cloth or paper. Place this marker high up so you can see it from a distance. Use the reference marker to get your bearings should you have trouble finding the trail.

Now examine the spot where the deer was standing when shot for blood, hair, or your arrow (if it was not seen striking the animal). If there is blood, determine its color and amount (spotty or heavy).

If the archer cannot find his arrow nor any blood, he should go back to the spot he shot from and shoot another arrow to the spot where the deer was standing. If he missed the deer, he should be able to find the first arrow somewhere near the second. If not, then he must assume that the deer was hit. If he finds the arrow, it must be checked carefully for blood or hair.

Assuming that you have made a hit, the next step is to locate the wounded deer.

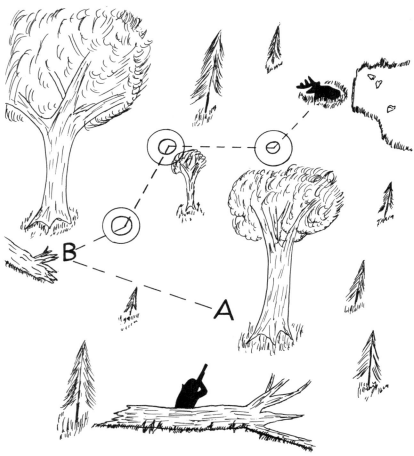

Location *A* is the spot where the deer was standing when shot. Location *B* is the spot where the deer was last seen. ----- is the path the deer took. Concentric circles represent circles made by the hunter to locate blood trails.

First, mark the first spot of blood you see with an arrow or brightly-colored paper (toilet paper is popular). Or use another hunter as a marker. He can help you locate the trail and keep an eye out for the deer in case it gets up.

Next, follow the blood trail—but do not walk on the trail! Walk off to the side to preserve it. You may need even a minute drop to find the trail should it suddenly end.

Always track slowly, as if you were stalking the game—which is what you are actually doing. Be ready in case the wounded deer suddenly appears. This is especially important if the blood trail is thin or spotty.

When looking for blood, check the sides of trees and bushes on the side the wound would brush against. Place a marker at each change in direction and if the trail is spotty, place a marker at each new finding. The markers should be placed so they can be seen at a distance.

Try to notice any unusual characteristics the tracks have such as a limp or dragging foot or abnormal hoof markings. Note their size. This is useful if your deer crosses another's trail.

On several occasions I have seen a blood trail from another wounded deer mix with the one I was following. Without knowing track characteristics, I could have followed the wrong deer.

If you push a wounded deer from his bed, wait at least an hour before resuming tracking, for you now can assume that he was not hit as seriously as you first thought.

If the trail ends, mark the last spot of blood and using it as a starting point walk around it in an outward spiral, moving out another three feet with each complete turn. If, after making at least 10 circles, nothing turns up, go back to the last marker and take another trail. Repeat the spiral routine again. You may have to do this several times before locating additional sign.

Should circling fail, look for signs other than blood. The wounded deer is in a hurry and probably a bit wobbly from loss of blood. In his haste he kicks up leaves and bumps into small branches, breaking some off. By staying low, the hunter can see where the leaves have been disturbed. When tracking, keep the trail between you and the sun. At this angle, sunlight brings out details much better.

If the track has a severe drag mark, indicating a limp or a broken leg, the deer will stay on level ground. Otherwise he usually heads downhill or toward a body of water. If for some reason you are unable

Slow, careful tracking will pay off.

to locate the deer by the end of the day, try picking up the trail near a body of water. He may head there to throw you off his trail, and he will seek water to cool the fever he received from the wound.

Often wounded deer are accompanied by other deer. If you jump a deer while following a blood trail, don't assume it is the wounded deer. Make a mental note of where the new deer ran, but follow the blood trail you are on. Follow the new deer only if your trail runs out.

With persistence, care, and knowledge you can find your deer.

APPROACHING A WOUNDED DEER

When you find your deer, approach with caution. Deer have extraordinarily strong legs and can injure you by kicking.

One of the first deer I bagged gave me a scare I won't soon forget. I had a single-shot shotgun and two old shells of No. 4 buckshot. I was sitting on a board nailed between two trees when I noticed a six-

Deer in a hurry, especially when wounded, will turn leaves over, leaving a visible trail. If you lose the blood trail, you can often use the turned leaves and broken branches to find your deer.

point buck walking straight at me. As he stopped from time to time to check behind him, I got set to take aim.

When he got within 20 yards he gave me a broadside profile and I fired. The deer went down but struggled to get up. I quickly broke open the gun and put in the other shell, aimed, and pulled the trigger. A loud "click" was the response. The old shell just didn't want to do its job.

I quickly ran over to the deer and called my cousin who was only some 80 yards away. As I reached the deer it had just about regained its footing. I grabbed his antlers and laid my body—which only weighed about 135 pounds then—across its back in hope of putting him back down.

It didn't work out that way. The deer took off with me laying across his back like a saddlebag, headed for an open field 30 yards away. I held onto my prize until I saw a barbed wire fence just a few yards ahead. At that time I figured I had better part company and did so just as the deer dove through the strands!

As I watched the deer collapse just 20 yards from the fence I could hear my cousin laughing to the point of tears. It was funny, but I was lucky too. The buck could just as easily have gored me with his antlers.

23

Field Dressing

The key to good-tasting wild meat is a quick kill and fast cooling. Field dressing is the most important step in this process.

If your animal is dead, it serves no purpose to try to bleed it, because its heart has stopped and will not pump any blood. Trying to bleed at this point disfigures the cape—not good if you intend to have the animal mounted.

When field dressing any hoofed game, place the animal's head slightly uphill—or at least level with the rest of the body. This makes removing the organs easier when the time comes for that step. Some hunters like to rig a tripod or lever so that the animal is in an upright position, but I find that to be unnecessary work. You can finish field dressing in less time than it takes to assemble the rig.

Next roll the deer onto his back. If he is too heavy to roll, tie a length of rope to his legs on one side and use a nearby tree as a pulley. Secure him with the rope.

Some hunters immediately remove the tarsal glands located at the inside of the rear leg joints (hocks) because they believe they affect the taste of the meat. Neither I nor any of my hunting associates have

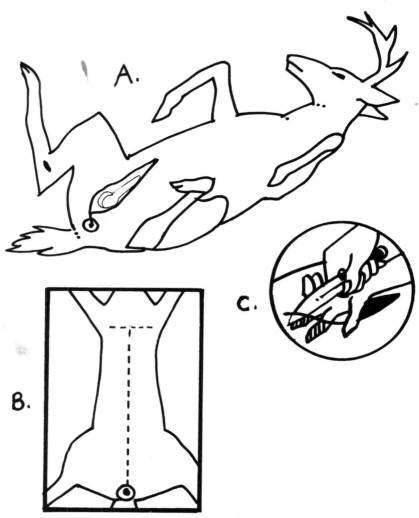

A. Place the deer on its back. If starting from the bottom, remove the genitals and cut around the anus.

B. Lines indicate where to cut.

C. Once the skin layer is cut, use your finger to guide the blade to prevent cutting any of the internal organs.

found this to be true. We have found that in removing the glands before dressing you may transmit the strong odor to the meat with hands or knife. If you wish to remove the glands, I suggest you wait until you are finished hog-dressing and cleaning out the body cavity.

There are two ways to dress a deer: from the chest to the anus, or from the anus to the chest. I find it easier to work from the anus up.

Start by fleshing out the genitals by grasping them in one hand and cutting the skin all around them without cutting into the abdominal wall. Cut the penis free from the pelvic arch.

Continue the cut around to the anus base of the tail. The anal area is made up of pliable but tough tissue, so a sharp knife is a must. Cut around the vent without cutting into it, then carefully insert your knife and cut around (ream) the vent until it is free and can be pulled out far enough to be tied in a knot (or with a string if you have one). This will prevent stool from being dropped into the body cavity when the intestines are removed.

After the vent has been prepared, insert two fingers under the skin and muscle of the lower abdomen and lift it away from the intestines. Your fingers serve as a guide to keep the intestines from being cut by your knife blade as you cut toward the top of the body cavity. If you are going to save the cape for mounting, you should stop cutting when you reach a point between the two front legs.

The benefit of having the head uphill is now apparent. Gravity pulls the insides toward you and exposes the diaphragm.

The diaphragm is a strong layer of muscle that separates the chest cavity from the abdominal cavity. This is where the job gets messy, especially if you have shot through the rib cage. Reach into the cavity with your knife and cut the diaphragm loose from the rib cage. It is best to start at the top and make sweeping strokes down both sides toward the spine. As you do this you feel the contents begin to come loose from the cavity.

With the diaphragm removed, roll the deer onto his side and spill the contents out onto the ground. A few more cuts around the vent may be necessary to free it. Some cutting may also be needed to free the bladder from the pelvic area. Be careful here: gently grasp the bladder with one hand and pull it outside the body cavity, then cut it free. If any urine enters the cavity, immediately and thoroughly wipe it clean.

Some people split the pelvic bone to clean out that area further. However, if you reamed the vent properly this will not be needed. I have found that splitting the pelvic bone only results in the drying out of the precious meat. If you decide to split the pelvic bone, it may be necessary to use a small hatchet or a cleaver. Your knife may be a bit too light to do the job safely.

The next step is to reach into the chest cavity and remove any of the remaining debris. Reach up as far as you can and remove as much of the windpipe as possible. You won't have much room up there, so watch how you use the knife.

The final step is to turn the deer onto its belly and let the blood drain. While the blood is draining, salvage the heart and liver. I carry a plastic bag for this purpose. When the cavity has drained for a while, turn the deer back on its back and wipe the cavity clean.

In warm weather, flies materialize from out of nowhere to lay their eggs in the meat. When the larva hatch they will feed on it. It is advisable to cover the deer with cheesecloth. Another very effective method is to give all the exposed areas a good dusting with black pepper. Pepper is a good fly repellent and it doesn't affect the taste of the meat to any large degree. Should flies get to your deer, wash the larvae out as soon as possible.

24

Transporting the Deer

After the field dressing is over and you have cleaned yourself up a bit, the next task is to get the deer back to camp. Depending on the size of the deer, the physical condition of the hunter, and the terrain, this can be quite easy or nearly impossible.

The easiest way to take a deer out of the woods is with the aid of another hunter. Tie the hooves together and run a stout pole between the legs. Two hunters can then easily carry the deer out of the woods.

If help is unavailable, the best way to carry the deer is over your shoulders. Dead weight isn't easy to pick up, so make sure you're in shape. Be sure to tie all four hooves together so they won't catch on the brush. This also makes the deer easier to carry. Tie a brightly-colored cloth on the antlers and tail to avoid being shot at by some novice as you walk through the woods.

If carrying the deer out is impossible, the next best way, if you have to go quite a distance, is to build a travois. A travois is merely two poles secured at one end giving it the shape of a V. Cross members are added to maintain this shape and to support any items placed upon the travois. If you use this method you will find much easier going if you place most of the weight near the bottom. Grasp the two poles so that the point drags on the ground.

Drag the deer out only if you are not worried about the condition of the hide. Rocks and debris pull the hair out and sometimes cut into the flesh. If you decide to drag the deer and want to save the head for a mount, tie one end of a rope around the base of both antlers. Then run the rope to the snout and secure it with a loop. Tie the other end of the rope to a short, stout stick that serves as a handle. This will keep the head off the ground while you drag the deer.

Unless you are going downhill or there is snow on the ground, dragging dead weight is no fun. Take it slow and avoid brushy areas and blowdowns whenever possible. Deer trails are best to use if a road or fire cut is not available.

For some, even dragging is too much—especially if the deer weighs more than 200 pounds. In this instance it is best to build a tripod with long stout poles and hang the deer until you can come back with help. This also gives the deer a chance to drain.

Tie the poles, which should each be over eight feet long, together at one end then spread the poles in a triangular shape. Tie a rope loosely around the base of the antlers (the neck if it's a doe). Make sure the knot won't slip. Place the loosely-tied rope at the antler base over the tied ends of the tripod. Pushing up one pole at a time, you will be able to raise the deer off the ground.

Another method is to use leverage. With this method you need only one strong pole of about 10 feet and three pieces of rope.

Simply tie a line around the pole about three quarters of the way from one end. Tie the other end of the line to a branch about eight feet above the ground. Next tie a long piece of rope to the end of the long section of the pole. Tie the short end of the pole to the antler base (or neck of a doe). Last, simply return to the long end of the pole and pull the long end of it down and hoist the deer up into the air. Once raised, secure to a near-by tree or to the tree you are using to hoist the deer up. You will find that with this method you can lift game twice as heavy as you are.

If there are other hunters in the area and you are afraid to leave your deer hanging in the woods, your only alternative is to bury the deer under leaves (which will probably spoil the meat) or pack it out (see BUTCHERING).

When it comes time to transport the carcass home, there are a

By using leverage you can lift a deer twice your weight.

few things to remember. The carcass must be kept cool and well ventilated. Never tie a deer to the hood of a vehicle—engine heat will destroy the taste of the meat. Never lock it in the trunk of a car—if you must use the trunk, leave it open at least one foot. Ventilation from heat and exhaust fumes are a must.

25

Skinning

If a cooler (or butcher) is not available, skinning should be done as soon as possible, preferably as soon as you get back to camp.

First, hang the deer. I prefer to hang mine by the hind legs. Cut off all four legs at the knee joint, then make a cut through the skin above the hind leg joints.

Next, insert the end of a stout rope through the hole in the leg and tie a knot. After both hind legs have been thus secured, hoist the deer up in such a way that the rear legs are spread apart and high enough so you can easily work on them.

Using a sharp knife, split the hide from the base of the tail to the end of the leg joint, then open the skin on the inside of the forelegs to the brisket. At this point you must peel the skin from around the legs to the main body. Careful knife work is a must here.

If you are going to save the head for mounting, make your cuts on the cape now (if you haven't already removed it), so it won't be damaged when you remove the hide. If you are not going to save it, continue to split the hide from the rib cage to the jaw.

At this point, if you wish to save the tail, make a lengthwise cut from the underside of the tail halfway to the end of the tail. This allows you to grasp the tail bone and pull it loose from the skin.

It is mostly muscle power from here on. Tightly grip the freed hide and pull down. From time to time, you may have to punch the meat to free the hide. A little knife work on stubborn areas may be necessary.

If you're not saving the head, it can be easily severed by cutting through the meat and severing the first vertebra (the Atlas). After that, cut all the way around the neck to free the head. Removing the head this way preserves the valuable stewing meat on the neck.

A second, and faster, way to remove the hide is popularly known as the ''golf ball'' method. This procedure works best with the deer hanging by its head.

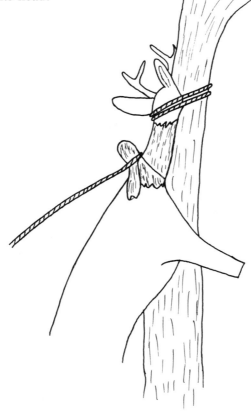

The Golf-Ball Method: Secure a rock about the size of a golf ball under the skin at the back of the neck. Make slits as described in text. Sever legs at hock and knee joints.

First, sever the legs at the knee joint and the hind legs at the hock. Then split the hide from the end of the legs to the main body. Continue this split from the brisket to the jaw. Again, if you are going to save the cape, make the necessary cuts now.

Peel the neck skin back, then insert a round stone about the size of a golf ball beneath the hide, so that you can tie a rope around it and the skin to form a large "knot."

Now simply attach the other end of the rope to a vehicle and drive away. The skin comes off without damaging the meat. In warm weather flies and yellowjackets will immediately locate your deer, making skinning difficult without being stung at least once. Under such conditions you will appreciate this convenient method.

THE CAPE

Once in a while a hunter bags a spectacular deer, or one which has special meaning to him, and wants to have it mounted. Careful removal of the cape is extremely important for mounting.

If the weather is warm and you can't get the deer to a taxidermist within 18 hours of killing him, it is your responsibility to remove the cape quickly to prevent spoilage and hair loss. A word of caution here: don't trust this job to a butcher or food processor. Many hunters have learned that lesson too late, including me.

When I bagged my first buck I wanted to immortalize him. I took him to a butcher to have the cape removed so I could then take it to a taxidermist. When the butcher was finished, the cape was much too short and damaged in all the critical places. From that time on I have made it a point to do all my skinning myself, and to learn the proper way to remove the cape. After consulting a few cooperative taxidermists, I have found that it is not really hard to do—in fact cape removal and skin preparation is now quite easy.

You need four pieces of equipment to cape out your trophy. The first is a camera—yep, I said a camera! It serves two purposes: it helps you remember the special event, and it serves as a guide for the taxidermist. Pictures help the taxidermist do a much better job of duplicating the head the way it originally appeared.

Film is cheap, so shoot as many close-up shots of the head as you can. Be sure to snap several different views—top, sides, frontal, etc. Capture all the features of the head.

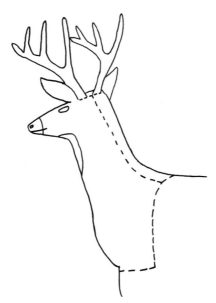

On all antlered animals the cape should be cut along these lines.

The second piece is a knife with a blade that need be no longer than four inches. I have found that a slightly dull knife reduces the chance of accidental cuts through the skin.

The third piece is a saw; this is needed only to remove the antlers from the skull.

The fourth piece is a screwdriver: it is used to remove the hide from around the antler bases.

The first cut should be from the withers (top of the shoulders) straight down to the middle (or just behind) the shoulder and across it in a direct line to a point 6–8 inches below the brisket, to a line between the forelegs. Continue the cut completely around and back up to the starting point at the withers.

Next split the hide from the withers up through the back of the neck to the center of the top of the head, between the antler bases. Then make a cut from that point to the antler base on each side.

Now peel the hide off the shoulders and both sides of the neck and skin out the brisket section, up to the throat. Remove as much fat as possible from the hide as you work.

Cut six inches behind brisket point.

At this point, remove the wind pipe if you haven't already. When doing so take care not to get blood on the white skin of the throat. If it dries it may stain the hair.

You have a choice of how you want to work from here. You can either remove the head (by severing the Atlas joint) or leave it on. Most taxidermists prefer to remove the head.

The ears are next—but take it slow! This is another area for a dull knife. Sever the ear cartilage about ½ inch below the outside opening of the ear.

Use a screwdriver to free the skin around the antlers. Work the point slowly all the way around each antler base.

From now on, be extra careful to ensure a good, mountable cape.

As you work from the antlers toward the eyes, stick a finger under the eyelid and stretch it forward to expose the adjoining tissue. This prevents you from cutting into the lid. Caution! A slip here can greatly damage the head's appearance.

The tear ducts located beneath the eyes should be skinned close to the bone, keeping the skin whole.

When you work your way to the mouth, leave about one inch of

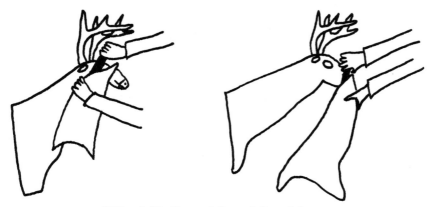

With a dull knife, carefully work toward the nose.

the inner skin so the taxidermist will have more to work with when modeling the face.

The nostrils can be cut free but, as with the mouth, leave about a one-inch margin.

Removing the antlers. With the cape free, you can now remove the antlers from the skull. Using the saw, cut from about midway between the eye sockets and continue through the middle of the ear butt.

With the skin and antlers free, remove all excess fat and meat you can find with the knife. Again, be careful not to cut through the

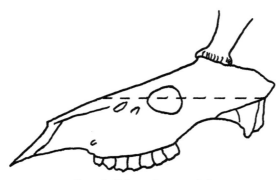

Saw skull through eye socket.

skin as you flesh it out. Turn the ears inside out and carefully remove the cartilage. If you find that to be a bit tricky, just salt them down—as you will the rest of the skin—and save cartilage removal for the expert.

Salting the hide.   Granular salt works best and should be worked into every roll and crack of the hide. Pay particular attention to the mouth and nostrils: some taxidermists advise making small slits in the tissue of these areas so that the salt will penetrate, preventing spoilage and hair loss.

The salted cape should be spread out and kept away from the sun and heat for 24 hours—or at least rolled up, flesh side in.

Then the salting process should be repeated and the hide allowed to dry and drain some more. This preserves the skin and makes it lighter for travel and—if needed—shipping.

Shipping the hide.   If you want to ship your cape and hide, some small but important rules should be observed. Don't tie the hide with wire or colored string, as they may stain the hide. The hide should be shipped in a plastic bag inside a box or crate. The bag will keep the liquids leeched out by the salt from leaking through the box. If the box breaks because of leakage, you may never see your cape and hide again.

If you have a good taxidermist, your care in preparing the cape and hide will be rewarded with a true-to-life mount that lasts a lifetime.

DEER WEIGHT AND MEAT CALCULATIONS

You may wonder later how much your deer weighed when it was alive, or how much meat you will get from it. A few simple calculations help answer those questions.

Experts differ on the base figure for finding live weight from dressed weight. Some multiply field-dressed weight by 1.25, some use 1.275 or even 1.30.

Noted wildlife photographer, writer, and lecturer Leonard Lee Rue III gives—in his book *The Deer of North America* (page 115)—a figure slightly lower than 1.25 for use on big deer, because a small deer has more "innards" in proportion to its total body weight than a great big fellow does.

Considering the amount of research he has done on deer, and the recent tests I have made, I must agree with him.

Calculating meat weight.   To find how much meat you will get from your deer, you have to consider the butcher's skill and how much meat was damaged by the shot.

If you have left the bones in, simply divide the dressed weight by 4, then subtract the number you get from the dressed weight—or multiply the dressed weight by .75.

For example, if a deer dressed out at 150 pounds and was killed by a clean lung or heart shot, you will receive 112.5 pounds of meat (150 × .75 = 112.5).

If you decide to debone your deer—as I usually do when pressed for time—you end up with about 40 percent of the dressed weight in meat. For example, 150 pounds dressed weight yields about 60 pounds of meat. Deboning means less to pack out of the woods and saves room in the freezer.

26

Butchering

Everyone agrees that the most convenient way to turn a carcass into chops, steaks, and roasts is to take it over to the neighborhood butcher. However, in the age of supermarkets and stringent health codes, what few neighborhood butchers there are may be prohibited from working on your deer. Deer-butchering services charge a fee, and to many hunters it is worth it. They skin the deer, clean the meat, remove the hair, and then process the meat to your specifications. They double-wrap the meat and label the packages. What could be more convenient?

Unfortunately, there are a few slip-shod deer butchers around. The hunter may end up with someone else's deer or lose some meat. After harvesting scores of deer and processing most of them myself (with a trusted butcher), I know what my deer will taste like before it gets to the table, regardless of what it fed on.

During the past few years my butcher has been unavailable, so after bagging a deer I tried one of these deer butchers.

A week later they had it finished. When I picked it up the weight didn't seem right and I began to wonder. At dinner that evening I was positive the meat was not mine: it was strong to the point of being inedible.

Naturally there are butchers that are honest and good at their job, but you could be disappointed in the results unless you insist that you be present when the deer is being processed. That's a bit unusual, but you worked hard for that deer, and the money you are paying the butcher gives you that right.

Aging.   If at all possible, the deer should be aged for about three weeks at a temperature between 36 and 38 degrees before butchering. Hanging it outside in the elements won't do. Either the weather is too warm and the meat starts to spoil, or it's too cold and the meat won't age. The only positive way is to hang it in a cooler.

Well, I shouldn't have said "positive." Once the freezer's plug was pulled out by accident while I had my deer aging. A good butcher was able to save it, by washing it down with vinegar and wiping with a clean cloth. Vinegar takes away the slickness and the odor. If you are in doubt, a butcher can tell you if the meat has gone bad.

There is another way to age meat when you can't hang it because of warm weather or a lack of facilities. Let meat you intend to cook sit in the refrigerator for about three days at 36–38 degrees. Small cuts age much faster than the whole carcass. Steaks and chops, for example, age in about three days or so. A roast may take five. Remember to keep the meat covered so it doesn't dry out—especially if you have a frost-free refrigerator.

Butchering.   If you decide to butcher by yourself, you will need the proper tools to do a good job: a long butcher knife, a meat cleaver (a hatchet will do in a pinch), a boning knife, and a meat saw (a hacksaw is OK but use a wood saw only in a pinch). Meat hooks are handy, but in a jam use a stick to hold the hind legs apart.

You need a strong table. Don't use a painted table—I once used my painted table outside and found that meat has an adhesive quality. When I lifted the meat from the table, paint chips stuck to it. It may have been because the knife blade loosened some paint, but I cannot be sure.

Hang your deer high enough and securely so you can saw the carcass along the center of the backbone from one end to the other. Hose it down to remove all the dirt, hair, and other debris—contrary to popular belief, water does not harm the meat. Next, take a vinegar-

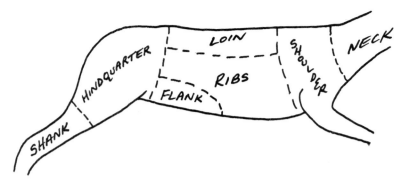

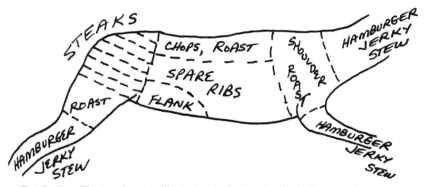

Butchering: The top drawing illustrates the basic cuts, the bottom popular uses.

soaked cloth and wipe it down. After allowing the carcass to drain for a few minutes, you are ready to begin.

First, remove all excess fat.

Next, split the carcass in half down the middle of the backbone. If you stay in the center of the bone you will find the cutting quite easy.

Sever the neck at the point where it joins the shoulder. The neck can be boned and cut up for stew meat, hamburger, or jerky.

Next, cut the front half from the rest of the deer. Cut just behind the shoulders, freeing the entire shoulder section.

Next, cut the midsection from the hindquarters starting at the high point of the backbone. Again, you need the saw. Cut off the flank meat and separate the ribs from the loin.

Table butchering.   You now have the basic cuts and can proceed to chop, saw, and cut them into cooking size. Cut across the grain and not with the grain. It makes meat much easier to chew.

The hindquarters are relatively small and should be cut into steaks one inch or thicker. I prefer two inches. However, some people like to cut a roast from the bottom half. The lower part of the hindquarter—the shank—is great for deerburgers and stew meat.

The loin can be removed in a long strip and made into tasty roasts by boning it along the backbone. This is the way most people, including myself, prefer. Cut thick and stuffed, they melt in your mouth.

You can also make loin chops by cutting through the meat to the backbone, then carefully chopping through the backbone with either a cleaver or a hatchet. If you are not very handy with a cleaver, place the blade where you want to cut and lightly pound the top with a piece of wood, mallet, or maul.

The shoulder can be cut into steaks, but I prefer to have the entire shoulder, except for the shank, cut into three roasts. I have the shank cut into stew meat or ground up for deerburgers.

For some unknown reason, ribs are often discarded. If people knew how delightful they are when barbecued, you can bet they would never throw them away again. The ribs should be cut in squares of about four inches. Use the cleaver to cut across the ribs and a knife to separate the rib squares.

Wrapping.   Wrapping the meat is an important step. Use heavy-weight freezer wrap with a wax or plastic coating. Wrap to keep out air—double wrap each portion and seal tightly.

Label each piece with a marker or adhesive sticker.

During the butchering you no doubt cut out the blood-filled areas, usually the shoulder or ribcage. If there isn't too much shattered bone in that area, you can probably save some meat. Bloodshot meat is where the arrowhead or bullet caused damaged veins to clot, and soaking the bloodshot meat in cold water washes away the blood. In most cases, the meat is as good as the other portions.

Burgers, sausage, and jerky.   Some hunters take meat they have set aside for burgers and mix it with pork or hamburger. The ratio is usually one pound of pork or beef to four pounds of venison.

Others take stew and burger meat to the butcher and have sausage made from them. A good butcher can work wonders and it is worth the modest price they usually charge.

The flank makes great jerky and you can do it in your home. Simply cut the flank into long strips of about one inch wide, then lace them with salt, pepper, or flavored steak sauce or barbecue sauce. Drape them over the oven racks and heat them to 150 degrees until hard and dry. It takes about seven hours but this treat is well worth it.

27

Trophy Hunting

If you are looking for a whitetail that will take a high spot in the Boone and Crockett Club, your chances are getting slimmer every year. However, regions around the Black Hills of South Dakota are consistent producers of nice heads, and will probably remain so. Saskatchewan produces some of the most spectacular heads you will ever see, the only problem being that Saskatchewan game officials often restrict U.S. sportsmen. If you do get a chance to hunt there, the southeastern part of the province is the place to go. Another highly rewarding area to hunt is the northeast section of Montana. New Brunswick may well be the next producer of a top ranking head. There the average buck harvested is 4.5 years old and will dress out at 205 pounds and support racks with 10 points with a 120-mm beam circumference. The fact that their herd is increasing offers encouragement.

Hunters who would like to bag a trophy-class buck have two ways to go about it: they can depend on luck when hunting a new area, or can do some hard work.

A hunter who is serious about bagging a big buck must communicate with wildlife departments in the states he hunts. You should find out the average of dressed-weight deer taken in an area; from that you can estimate the average size.

You should determine the average age of harvested deer. If it is under 3½ years, your chances of bagging a trophy-size buck are slim at best. The hunting pressure is probably very high.

Ask these questions of an area you are considering visiting:

Is the deer population rising, falling, or constant? Poor habitat and poor management are indicated by a steady decline in population and mean fewer big bucks.

Are license sales rising or declining? If declining, this indicates that local hunters are not happy with hunting conditions and are spending their time and money elsewhere. One reason for a decline is a lack of prime hunting habitat. Crowded conditions are no fun and certainly not for the serious hunter.

Take my home state for example. There is very little public hunting land and what there is is overcrowded. To make matters worse, virtually all the private deer habitat is posted or controlled by private hunting clubs.

Ask game officials where the best hunting areas are. Pick one of the top three. If one of the areas should also offer the hunter mule deer, your chances of finding a large buck has increased. Hunters that have a choice between the mule deer and the whiletail will usually choose to hunt the easier-to-harvest mule deer. This gives the crafty whitetail a chance to mature.

Find out if there have been any major timber harvests or burnoffs during the last few years. If so, head for that area—if the population there is growing.

Find out the average rack size. Size varies greatly from area to area, and this information, if reliable, can be a deciding factor.

Find out how much public hunting land is available to the non-resident hunter and where you can find information on securing a place to hunt.

Guides.   If the area you have chosen is quite a distance away and you won't have a chance to prescout, ask if there are guides for that area. If you are going to spend your time and money to travel for a trophy deer, it makes sense to use a guide who can scout for you.

Thoroughly check a guide's references.

Once a gunning club I used to belong to hired a guide at the last minute. He and his partner were the biggest rip-offs I have ever come across. Neither would walk deeper than 25 yards from a road and, for some reason, they kept blowing a whistle as they walked. Apparently they were afraid of getting lost or shot. It was obvious why they were "available" at the last minute.

When you select a guide, tell him what you want, how you hunt, and what your experience is. A reputable guide won't tarnish his hard-earned reputation with false claims. He'll be honest enough to tell you if he knows there are exceptional deer in his area and if the probability of taking one is high.

The hardest part comes when you are in the woods hunting the elusive whitetail. Sacrifice! Pass up all the easy-to-get young bucks which present themselves to you. During the first 1½ years a buck isn't much smarter than a box of rocks. This is one reason for their high harvest rate. The temptation to take one is great. Some will have fair-sized racks. Unless you are allowed two bucks, pass them up. Often the biggest deer are taken on the last day of the hunt.

28

Backpacking and Camping for Deer

Backpacking for whitetails is becoming increasingly popular, especially early in the season and in warmer climates. Backpacking hunters want to get away from the crowds and perhaps nail an exceptional buck or at least an early deer.

Backpackers know the value and necessity of traveling light and using proper equipment.

Pack. A backpacker on the move for a couple of days may carry over 35 pounds of equipment. Use a rigid packframe—either the external or internal kind. These keep the weight over your feet, reducing fatigue and discomfort. Packs without a frame carry the weight too low and too far away from your back, causing excess pull on your shoulders. You will be walking in an awkward, leaning posture to compensate for the poor weight distribution. A waist strap to anchor the frame to your hips transfers most of the weight to the stronger hip and leg muscles. The best feature of a rigid frame pack is that it can carry the additional weight of a butchered deer.

The pack must be packed correctly. Keep such light items as

clothes, dried foods, and sleeping bag on the bottom and such heavier items as tent, raingear, water, cooking utensils, and first aid kit on top. The higher the weight the easier your travels. Keep items that you may want quickly in one of the side pouches.

Sleeping bag. You will spend a third of your time in your sleeping bag. A poor choice will mean long, cold, sleepless nights . . .

Filler. The top filler material choice is new down. Down is lighter than other fillers and can be compressed better—a definite plus. Down makes as warm a bag as you can find. New down retains all body heat because it traps air, yet it breathes—circulates air and prevents dampness inside the bag. It is both fire retardant and waterproof. Ounce for ounce, a down bag is the best camping investment you can make. Beware of reprocessed down and feather bags, however; they are not as warm or comfortable.

Polyester fiberfill sleeping bags are my second choice. They are nearly as warm as and less expensive than down bags, but do not have the other advantages of down bags.

Acetate fiber is not as warm or as fluffy as down or fiberfill. A good wool blanket should be used with this type of bag.

Maintenance. A good bag is expensive and requires some attention from time to time. Air the bag out frequently. Use a waterproof ground cloth to protect it from wear and moisture—an air mattress also works well. Have it dry cleaned. Work the zippers easily and lubricate them regularly with soap and a thin coat of light oil.

The tent. A tent used in cold weather should be made airtight to hold body heat. A windproof and waterproof tent is useless if pitched too loosely because the air moves around inside it, robbing the hard-earned body heat. Secure it well.

A single backpacker wants a light, one- or two-man tent—or just a ground cloth. A group of men staying a few days or more will need a tent high enough to stand in and large enough to hold all of their gear.

HUNTER'S BARE NECESSITIES CHECK LIST.

____ Air mattress or ground cloth

____ Axe

____ Binoculars

____ Camera and film

____ Candles

☑ Canteen or water bag
___ Compass and map
___ Deer bag or cheesecloth
☑ Detergent
___ Extra blanket
☑ " boots
☑ " clothing
___ " wool socks
___ " wool shirts
☑ " gloves
___ First aid kit
☑ Food
☑ Flashlight and batteries
☑ Knife
☑ License
___ Lip balm

___ Medicine
___ Nailclipper
☑ Pack and frame
☑ Plastic bags
___ Rain gear
___ Salt and black pepper
___ Saw
___ Sharpening stone
☑ Sleeping bag
☑ Stove
___ Sunglasses
☑ Tent and repair kit
☑ Watch
___ Water purifying tablets
☑ 50 feet of nylon rope
___ Tape measure

PERSONAL HYGIENE
___ Tooth brush and paste
☑ Face cloth
☑ Towel

☑ Toilet paper
☑ Soap

WEAPONS
___ Gun
___ Gun case
___ Cleaning kit
___ Repair kit
___ Ammunition
___ Scope/lens covers
☑ Bow

☑ Extra string and cables
☑ Shooting glove
☑ Armguard
☑ Arrows
☑ Arrowheads
☑ Replaceable blades
___ Repair kit

EMERGENCY EQUIPMENT
___ Flares
☑ Mirror

___ Whistle
☑ Waterproof matches

KEEPING WARM

The most important equipment you carry into the field is your clothing. It is all that stands between your body and the harsh elements.

Each year more people venture into the wilderness to enjoy its beauty. Unfortunately, each year many are injured or die because they did not understand the importance of proper dress.

To help you understand the vital relationship between you, your clothing, and the environment, you must understand how your body works and how to protect it.

The vital organs within your body must remain at an even temperature, normally 98.6 degrees (F). Deviations of only a few degrees either way can cause illness and death. The body regulates its temperature by a process called homeostasis. When your body temperature rises, the blood vessels in your arms, legs, hands, and feet dilate to allow full blood flow to your skin surface. The heat dissipates through the skin.

When the body's temperature decreases the reverse occurs—blood flow to your toes and fingers can be cut by nearly 99 percent.

Your brain needs the oxygen that the blood carries in order to function properly. Homeostasis cannot totally cut off the blood supply to conserve heat. This is why as much as 50 percent of your body heat is lost from your neck and head.

By wearing a hat, you prevent a high percentage of body heat from escaping, thus allowing more blood to be sent to your fingers and toes.

Failure to keep your head and torso insulated will not only result in cold fingers and toes, it can cause hypothermia, and that my friend can kill you fast.

HYPOTHERMIA

Cold + wind + wetness + fatigue = hypothermia.

Hypothermia is caused by the loss of body heat at a rate faster than the rate it is produced by your body.

Strangely enough, most cases of hypothermia occur in seemingly mild 30–50 degree temperatures. Because few people recognize hypothermia until it has reached the advanced stages, most of the fatalities occur only 30–90 minutes after the first symptoms have developed.

Eating and exercising to produce body heat helps prevent hypothermia. Another preventative measure is conserving body heat with correct clothing (layered). The ideal clothing is adaptable to changing weather and activity levels, and allows body moisture to breathe away while preventing rain and snow from entering.

Some of the factors that cause hypothermia are: poor condition, inadequate nutrition and hydration, getting wet, exhaustion, thin build, nonwoolen clothing, and inadequate protection from wind, rain, and snow.

Signs.   Observed by others: poor coordination, stumbling, slowing of pace, amnesia, thickness of speech, hallucinations, irrationality or poor judgment, blueness or puffiness of skin, loss of contact with environment, stupor, weak or irregular pulse, decreased heart and respiratory rate, dilation of pupils.

Symptoms.   Felt by self: intense shivering, muscle tensing, feeling of deep cold or numbness, fatigue, poor coordination, stumbling, poor articulation (thickness of speech), disorientation, decrease in shivering followed by rigidity of muscles, blueness or puffiness of skin, slow or irregular or weak pulse.

Prevention.   Good rest and nutrition prior to climb or activity, continued intake of food, waterproof-windproof clothing, emergency bivouac equipment, early bivouac in storms, exercise to keep up the body's heat production such as isometric contraction of the muscles.

Treatment.   Slow reduction of heat loss. Shelter the victim from wind and weather and insulate him from the ground. Replace his wet clothing and put on windproof and waterproof outer gear. Make him move his limbs if possible.

Put the victim into a sleeping bag with another person. Have him huddle with the other person for body heat or give him hot drinks to warm him slowly. There is some disagreement on using hot water bottles or immersing the victim in a tub of hot water (110 degrees [F]) for severe cases. In the early stages of hypothermia this is considered safe.

What not to do.   Never try to rub heat back into a hypothermia victim. Never use *hot* water in the advanced stages. Never give alcohol to a victim. Never use fire as a source of heat.

All these methods cause a sudden rush of cold blood from the surface blood vessels to the inner core of the body. The core already is too cold and the new blood lowers the temperature even more. In some instances the process could be fatal.

DRESSING FOR WARMTH

Proper dressing as well as common sense eliminates hypothermia in all but severest weather.

There is a basic way of dressing properly: layers.

The layer closest to your body should trap your body heat and let your body breathe as well. It must permit body moisture to escape. Woolen mesh underwear or long johns are best for the first layer. I pick wool because it acts like a wick. By this I mean that it draws moisture away from the skin, yet keeps me warm even when it is wet from rain or perspiration. The net pattern traps the air but lets your body breathe.

Some people can't stand the feel of wool against their bodies. In this case a thin cotton or synthetic garment can be put on first. However, one must remember that cotton absorbs moisture and may contribute to hypothermia.

The next layer should be a light or medium-weight wool shirt—at least 80 percent wool is best—and trousers. For hunting, wool is again preferred for its insulating properties and because it is silent. Canvas trousers and cotton jeans make quite a bit of noise when rubbed together and in brush.

A wool or fiber-filled hat and a wool scarf or dickey are essential. Wool socks—80 percent or better—should always be worn. Have an extra pair available.

Layer three depends on how actively you hunt. If you walk a lot and the weather is not very cold, a down or fiberfilled vest may be all you need. A vest is easily stowed in your pack and can be left partly open as you walk.

If you do little exercise while hunting and the weather is cold, the third layer should include a full parka and possibly a pair of down trousers.

Gloves or mittens are a must. Nylon-finger-tipped gloves are a poor choice. I used a pair of them once and nearly suffered a frost-bitten index finger.

Layer four is for wind and rain. It doesn't take much of these two to bring on a good chill. Wear a windbreaker or shell. The important thing here is to let your body breathe. If it doesn't you will get wet from perspiration as well as from the rain—and be much colder.

This may seem like a lot of clothes but remember: once in the woods you can always remove some. You can't add clothing you don't have with you. I'll take warm over cold any day.

29

Outdoor Emergencies

Emergencies occur when you least expect them and are least prepared. If you know how to react, you can save yourself or a friend. This is particularly true in wilderness areas when help is not available.

Panic. The biggest problem an outdoorsman must overcome in an emergency is panic. Panic is a reflex to some people. For example, suppose you are doing some preseason scouting and you get tired. You walk to a nearby log and sit down. Suddenly you realize that a rattlesnake is sunning himself on the other end, just a few feet away. As an outdoorsman you may know that he can strike only two-thirds the length of his body and that you should either wait until he moves away or move away very slowly yourself.

However, your first impulse is to jump up and get out of there. You panicked.

Controlling panic takes conscious effort. When you realize that you are in a bad situation, force yourself to calm down and think. Never commit yourself to one course of action unless you have considered alternatives.

Lost.   One situation that pushes many outdoor enthusiasts' panic buttons is becoming lost. It happens to every outdoorsman at least once, and if you don't get a grip on yourself you can make it worse. Look at things logically. You walked in easily enough so the way out can't be that far off. You are not lost, you are just not very sure of where you are at the present time.

Sit down and breathe easy.

The next thing to do is analyze the situation. Ask youself questions like: Is help within walking distance? How far away is it? How is the weather? Do other people know you are in this area? When will they become concerned? Do you have food and water? Do you face starvation if you stay? Is there shelter? Is it better to use your energy to try to walk out?

If you decide to try to walk out, make some kind of written or mental note of your present location and in which direction you are going to head. As you walk, remember or mark down significant landmarks such as a deep ravine, sheer cliffs, streams, etc.

If you are in the mountains or hilly terrain, walk to a nearby top if it is not too high or far away. An extended view may yield a familiar sight: perhaps a road or building in the distance. Should the view offer nothing of encouragement, head downhill and look for a river or stream. Cabins and farms are often located close to a water source. The only drawback here is that water seldom goes in a straight line, so you may be in for a long walk.

Another way to guide yourself out is to remember where the sun was in relation to your trail when you entered the woods or the last time you knew where you were. This gives you the direction in which you were headed.

For example: In the northern hemisphere, if you walked into the woods in the morning and the sun was behind you, you were headed northwest. This is because the sun rises, during the autumn hunting season, in the southeast. The sun sets in the southwest. If you were sure you were walking in a generally straight line during the day, you can now make a fairly accurate guess as to which way to head back out. Since you *were* headed northwest, simply head southeast. Pick a distant landmark in that direction and head toward it. This won't take you back to your exact trail, but it will keep you from walking in circles and get you closer to your starting point.

Using a watch as a compass.   Should something happen to your compass, you can use your watch as a substitute. In the northern hemisphere follow this process: If your watch is set to Daylight Savings Time set it back one hour. Next, hold the watch level and hold a small stick or matchstick over the center of the watch. Turn the watch so that the stick's shadow falls on the hour hand. South will be directly between the hour hand and twelve if you make the reading between 6:00 a.m. and 6:00 p.m. Simply draw an imaginary line to the other side of the watch to find north.

If the time is between 6:00 p.m. and 6:00 a.m., the shadow will fall on north instead of south.

Using stars.　Using stars to find direction is easy. The usual way is to locate Polaris—the North Star. (Again, all instructions refer to the Northern Hemisphere.) On any clear night you can find the Big Dipper. The Big Dipper points to Polaris, which is located in the Little Dipper. The "pointers" should be familiar to any outdoorsman.

There is another way of using stars to find north, which can even be used on cloudy nights. Point a stick or gun at any star and keep it perfectly motionless. Lay or prop it against a stationary object. In a few minutes the earth's rotation moves the star from the point of aim. If the star rises you are facing east; if it descends, you are facing west. If it moves left you are facing north, and if it moves right, south.

Compasses.　If you have a compass—and all outdoorsmen should have at least one—your troubles are over (provided you remember in which direction you were headed when you entered the woods).

There are three types of compass. Each does the job if it is of good quality.

Type A compasses have a clockwise degree system which means that North is numbered zero and the numbers proceed to the right. All Type A compasses have a needle which operates independently of the compass card. (A compass card is the part of the compass which contains the markings in numbers, degrees, and N, S, E, and W.)

On a type B compass, the card and needle are joined and work as a unit. The most common of this type is the military lensatic type. It is designed to give only magnetic readings. By this I mean that the readings must be converted to True values in order to be useful in the field and to relate them to map bearings.

A type C compass simply has a counter-clockwise numbering system. The Forester compass is a popular model of this type.

Though compasses differ somewhat when used with maps, each is basically the same. They point to magnetic North and give false readings if metal objects are near by. Keep your gun a few feet away when using a compass.

There are books dealing specifically with compass reading and a wise outdoorsman will take the time to read one before going into the wilderness.

However, basic compass procedure that works without a map goes like this: decide in which direction you wish to travel and pick a landmark that is near your direction of travel. It should be as far in the distance as possible. Using the calibrated marks on the compass dial, note the number pointing to your landmark. Walk in that direction and check periodically to see that the number still lines up.

Staying put.   If you decide that staying put is a wiser choice, there are some very important guidelines to remember.

The most important element in survival is energy. To preserve energy you need shelter and warmth, and to replenish energy you must have food. This is no time to go on a diet.

To conserve energy, stay dry; wet clothes lose their insulating qualities. When the air chills your body, it draws off valuable energy reserves.

Another rule is Slow Down! When building a shelter or fire or locating food, slower movements burn less energy. Do not sweat. Perspiration means you are expending energy, and it makes you thirsty. You use up your water reserves. If you are thirsty, drink *warmed* liquids, as cold liquids take energy. Don't panic. The only thing that can harm you is fear.

Wild foods.   Eat whatever food is available. In whitetail country there are edible plants all around you. Learn to identify some before going hunting or wandering into the woods. Before eating wild food, perform this 4-part survival sequence: Smell, look, taste, wait.

Smell. If it has an odor, don't try it.
Look. If you can squeeze a milky substance from the plant, don't try it.
Taste. Bite off a small piece and place it on the inside of your

lower lip for about five minutes. If it doesn't taste bitter, burning, soapy, or foul, eat it.

Wait. After swallowing that small sample wait at least three hours for a reaction. If you experience no sickness or stomachache, it is safe to eat in bulk.

Unless you are an expert, leave all mushrooms alone.

Boil or bake whichever plants you eat. This makes them easier to digest, and better digestion means your body will extract more food value from the food.

Signal for help. Try not to use signals that soon become exhausted. Flairs, rockets, flashlights, and bonfires all have a limited life. They should be saved for when there is a good chance of rescue. If you use a bonfire, make three and set them in a triangular pattern. During daylight make fires as smoky as possible by piling on wet leaves, moss, or green wood.

At night make fires as bright and smokeless as possible.

Shelter. Shelter is available if you take the time to look for it. The lee side of cliffs, mountains, or large rocks and logs are your best protection from the elements.

Aside from a cave or rock overhang, the easiest, quickest, and least energy-burning shelter is a large downed tree. You can lean branches and logs along the trunk to form a crude roof. You can improve the roof by placing evergreen branches on top. This offers protection from the elements without costing much energy.

30

First Aid

This section is not intended to take the place of a first-aid manual. It does not presume to cover every situation. It is designed only to help you take care of common outdoor problems.

SHOCK

Shock is the first problem to deal with because it accompanies every injury. When the body is injured the nervous system is jolted, causing a sudden depression of bodily activities. Sometimes shock is more serious than the injury which caused it. Shock symptoms may not immediately arise. Depending on the individual's nervous system, it may take hours for them to be evident. When symptoms appear, treat at once.

Symptoms. The pulse is rapid and weak, the face pale, cold, and sweaty. Breathing may be shallow, irregular, and gasping. Some people have chills, others vomit or feel nauseated. Still others are disoriented. . .severe cases may lose consciousness.

Treatment. Apply heat to the body, but do not burn the victim. Wrap his body in anything that helps conserve his body heat. Apply some kind of heated object such as a hot-water bottle.

Lay the patient flat, then raise his legs higher than his head. If the victim has a head injury or nosebleed, however, keep him level.

Loosen all clothing to improve circulation.

Give the victim stimulants if he is conscious. Such hot liquids as tea are fine, but never give alcohol. Do not give stimulants if the victim has severe bleeding, a strong pulse, and a red face or a head injury.

WOUNDS

When the skin is broken you have two potential problems: infection and serious bleeding.

If bleeding is uncontrolled and in spurts, you may have to apply finger or hand pressure against a pressure point. Pressure points are

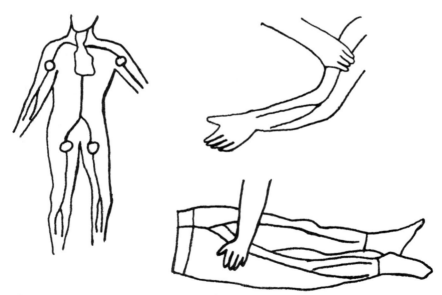

Pressure points: There are four points on the body where arterial pressure can be applied to someone with severe bleeding from the arm or leg. Firm pressure must be applied to restrict the bleeding.

places on the body where you can stop the flow of blood through an artery. Apply hand or finger pressure to the pressure point located between the heart and the injured area immediately.

Once the bleeding is under control, apply a form of antiseptic to the wound to kill germs, then securely apply a sterile dressing.

BURNS AND SCALDS

These common injuries are often treated incorrectly. When burns are extensive, you must also treat the patient for shock.

First-degree burns.   These show reddened skin. Cool the area as fast as possible with ice or cold water, then apply a burn ointment or baking-soda paste and cover with a sterile gauze pad. Don't use grease or butter.

Second-degree burns.   Here the skin is blistered. Treat as a first-degree burn, but don't break the blisters.

Third-degree burns.   This burn penetrates the skin completely and penetrates and destroys the epidermis and dermis. This kills the nerve endings in the skin, and thus the victim may feel less pain than in the case of a more superficial burn.

If help is immediately available, wrap the victim in clean sheets and a blanket and transport him to a hospital.

Should help not be immediately available, immerse the victim in water at room temperature until help arrives. This delays shock resulting from fluid loss. Do not wash, grease, powder, or medicate severe burns. Do not attempt to remove clothing from burned area. If the victim is conscious, give him fluids.

SPRAINS

Severe pain and immediate swelling over a joint are the normal symptoms of a sprain. Applied cold compresses and plenty of rest is the best treatment. Elevate the injured area whenever possible and have it checked for a possible bone fracture.

BROKEN BONES

A simple fracture may seem like a sprain in some cases. However, don't assume that no bones are broken merely because the victim can move the injured limb or joint.

Keep the patient warm and, if necessary, treat for shock. Treat the injured area with cold compresses and rest. Should a broken bone protrude through the skin and there be severe bleeding, stop the bleeding (see WOUNDS). Do not attempt to push the bone back into place or to clean the wound. This should be done by a physician.

Whenever the victim must be moved to receive medical attention, the fracture should be immobilized with splints to prevent further damage. Splints can be made from anything rigid enough to keep the broken bones from moving; branches, rolled-up magazines or newspapers, etc. The splints should be made long enough to reach beyond the joint both above and below the break. If possible, pad the splints with clean rags or clothing—cotton if possible. Tie the splints snugly but not tight.

Should the victim appear to have a broken or injured back or neck, don't move him or let him try to move. Keep the victim covered with blankets or coats where he lies. If moving the victim is absolutely necessary, move his body lengthwise, not sideways. A blanket or long coat should be slipped under him if possible so he can ride on that. Should the victim have to be lifted, keep his body in a straight line, don't jackknife him by lifting his head and heels only.

FROSTBITE

Frostbite is becoming increasingly rare, and thus hard to recognize. Frostbite not treated early can cost a limb. It pays to recognize the symptoms.

In the early stage of frostbite, there is a loss of feeling. The skin has a waxy appearance or maybe just some yellow-white spots. You will often see the danger before you feel pain. If the signs go unnoticed, the tissue may freeze solid without the victim being aware of it.

To fight frostbite you must keep yourself warm and maintain circulation. Slapping your face—or chewing—helps. Fingers and toes should be covered and kept moving.

If you become frostbitten, remember that the injured skin should be treated gently. Apply warm garments or body heat. For example, stick your hands between your legs or under your armpits. Apply tepid water to the area. Direct warmth from a lighter or campfire is dangerous because excessive heat increases tissue damage. Do *not* put snow on, or apply alcohol or kerosene to the affected area.

Once the skin thaws, exercise the affected parts and do not allow them to become frostbitten again for that may kill the tissues.

SNAKE BITE

Recently I was doing some preseason scouting during the summer and got a bit careless. While trailing a nice velvet-covered six-pointer, I nearly stepped on a copperhead. He struck at my boot but did not penetrate. At home, I brushed up on snakebite treatment.

If a poisonous snake bites you and injects venom, the two puncture wounds will almost immediately swell and turn red. If possible, send for a doctor immediately while you administer first aid.

The most important treatment is to remain calm and move as little as possible. The more you move, the faster the poison will reach your heart.

Most doctors agree that lancing and sucking out the poison is not the best way to treat snakebite. Most advise you to wipe the bitten area gently with a clean cloth and apply a firm bandage and a tourniquet between the wound and the heart. The bandage should be tight enough to retard the blood flow in the surface vessels, but not tight enough to stop circulation in the deep-lying vessels. Fluid will ooze from the wound if the bandage is adjusted properly. Apply ice or cold compresses to the bitten area. The tourniquet should be loosened for one minute every half hour. If ice or cold compresses are not present, use the snake-bite kit every outdoorsman should have.

Tie a bandage or tourniquet about three inches above the bite, between it and the heart. Take a sharp, sterile blade and make a short incision ¼-inch deep along the axis of the limb (don't make X shaped cuts) directly over each fang mark. Be careful not to cut an artery.

Next, apply suction to the wound with the suction cup in the snake-bite kit or your mouth. If you use your mouth, be sure you have no cuts or sores on your lips or mouth. Even though snake venom is not a stomach poison, your mouth should be rinsed with water, if possible. Continue the suction process for an hour or more. If available, cold compresses or ice should be applied for about two hours.

If sucking is not possible, follow the tourniquet and incision procedure and make the wounds bleed freely by squeezing the area manually.

It is also good to kill the snake to help the doctor determine the correct antidote.

Should the victim show signs of paralysis, he may soon stop breathing. If this happens, immediately administer artificial respiration.

Index